"Jesus' best-known command, 'Love one another,' is also the least obeyed. It's the most difficult thing Jesus asked us to do. Jerry Sittser doesn't make it any easier, but he shows how it is possible. He does it by embedding the love command in a network of New Testament 'mutuality commands' that support and nourish Jesus' command to love. This is accurate exegesis embraced by passionate concern and worked out in contexts in which any of us can recognize ourselves; the result is a book that will develop spiritual maturity in its readers and deepen the life of love in the church."

EUGENE H. PETERSON, PROFESSOR EMERITUS OF SPIRITUAL THEOLOGY, REGENT COLLEGE

Love One Another

BECOMING THE CHURCH JESUS LONGS FOR

Gerald L. Sittser

IVP Books

An imprint of InterVarsity Press
Downers Grove, Illinois

InterVarsity Press
P.O. Box 1400, Downers Grove, IL 60515-1426
World Wide Web: www.ivpress.com
E-mail: email@ivpress.com

Second edition ©2008 by Gerald L. Sittser

First published as Loving Across Our Differences ©1994 by Gerald L. Sittser

InterVarsity Press® is the book-publishing division of InterVarsity Christian Fellowship/USA®, a student movement active on campus at hundreds of universities, colleges and schools of nursing in the United States of America, and a member movement of the International Fellowship of Evangelical Students. For information about local and regional activities, write Public Relations Dept., InterVarsity Christian Fellowship/USA, 6400 Schroeder Rd., P.O. Box 7895, Madison, WI 53707-7895, or visit the IVCF website at <www.intervarsity.org>.

Scripture quotations, unless otherwise noted, are from the New Revised Standard Version of the Bible, copyright 1989 by the Division of Christian Education of the National Council of the Churches of Christ in the USA. Used by permission. All rights reserved.

Design: Cindy Kiple
Images: David Freund/iStockphoto

ISBN 978-0-8308-3449-5

Printed in the United States of America ∞

InterVarsity Press is committed to protecting the environment and to the responsible use of natural resources. As a member of the Green Press Initiative we use recycled paper whenever possible. To learn more about the Green Press Initiative, visit <www.greenpressinitiative.org>.

Library of Congress Cataloging-in-Publication Data

Sittser, Gerald Lawson, 1950-
  Love one another: becoming the church Jesus longs for / Gerald L.
Sittser.—[New ed.].
      p. cm.
  Rev. ed. of: Loving across our differences.
  Includes bibliographical references.
  ISBN 978-0-8308-3449-5 (pbk.: alk. paper)
  1. Church membership. 2. Love—Religious aspects—Christianity. 3.
Religious pluralism—Chrisitianty. 4. Multiculturalism—Religious
aspects—Christianity. 5. Christian life—Presbyterian authors. I.
Sittser, Gerald Lawson, 1950- Loving across our differences. II.
Title.
  BV4525.S58 2008
  250—dc22
                                                          2008002186

P   20   19   18   17   16   15   14   13   12   11   10   9   8   7   6   5

Y   24   23   22   21   20   19   18   17   16   15   14

In memory of my wife,

Lynda Dethmers Sittser,

whose life so wonderfully reflected

Jesus' commandment that

we love one another as he has loved us all.

Contents

Preface to the New Edition

For some reason I never reread the books I have written. By the time they are published, I ignore them because I am already working on some new project. It always comes as a surprise when, for whatever reason, I return to them after a five- or ten-year break. I always respond with a certain degree of ambivalence. I like the ideas; I don't always like the writing. I take it as a gift, therefore, when I can actually edit or rewrite those sections that fall short of the clarity and crispness I was hoping for but failed to achieve.

InterVarsity Press has given me this rare opportunity. In the early 1990s it published *Loving Across Our Differences*. Then, after spending fifteen years with other publishers, I happily returned to IVP to publish *Water from a Deep Well: Christian Spirituality from Early Martyrs to Modern Missionaries*. The editors suggested that *Loving Across Our Differences* be reissued, only under a new—and better—title, *Love One Another*. It gave me a chance to return to the book and revise it. What you have in your hands is the result of that effort.

I tried to update the book, largely because much has happened in my life—to say nothing about the world!—since the first edition was published. I changed some of the stories, eliminated others and cut sections that seemed redundant. My editor, Cindy Bunch, provided guidance along the way, and Kristi Reimer helped the process by working over the old edition first, making changes that improved the book significantly. I am deeply grateful for their efforts and support.

I finished writing the first edition in the aftermath of a tragic car accident that took the lives of my wife, Lynda, my mother, Grace, and my daughter Diana Jane. The accident plunged my family into a terrible darkness, bewildered us with unanswerable questions and left us with overwhelming responsibilities. Suddenly I found myself not only widowed but father to three very traumatized children (Catherine was eight at the time of the accident, David was seven and John was two).

This book, however, does not concern the accident. Instead, it focuses on the church, which, at least in our case, responded immediately and heroically to our predicament. Close friends rushed to my side and stayed there, as if permanently affixed to us. Kathy Bruner, the wife of a colleague, stayed with John, who was seriously injured, for three weeks at my home while he was in traction and later in a body cast. Ron and Julie Pyle provided childcare for John after he recovered from his injuries so that I could return to work, and Julie continued in that role for three years. The members of the university community and our home church worked together cooperatively to provide meals two or three times a week; in fact, some friends offered to do this for a whole year (though we chose, for the sake of settling into a normal routine, to decline). Thousands of people prayed faithfully for us, called to wish us well, and sent cards and letters. Counselors offered to meet with me and the children. Students volunteered to do yard work. The outpouring of support was unimaginable.

We experienced the church at its best. We were enveloped by the love of the body of Christ. I often found myself asking, "What would we do, where would we be, without the church?" Fellow believers comforted us, served us, bore our burdens and encouraged us. They fulfilled many of the mutuality commands that this book explores. They did not take the grief away; no one could do that. They did, however, make the grief more bearable. The tragedy and the events that followed showed me what the church is capable of doing.

What I believed when I wrote the first edition in the early 1990s has not changed at all. I still believe that the mutuality commands provide clear, concise and practical guidelines for Christian behavior in the church. They show us how to translate love from a vague sentiment into concrete action. I hope and pray that this short book will enable you to "make love your aim," as the apostle Paul puts it in 1 Corinthians 14, and thus turn his lofty vision of love, so beautifully expressed in 1 Corinthians 13, into a reality in your life, in the church and ultimately in the world.

1

The New Commandment

It is a phone call no parent wants to receive. "Jerry," Bethany said, "Catherine's had a little accident."

"Accident! How bad?"

"She's going to be okay. You want to talk to her? We're in a kind of ambulance crossing the Andes, headed down to Quito. Here she is."

My daughter Catherine and Bethany, one of her dear friends, spent the 2006-2007 school year in Central and South America, studying Spanish, traveling and serving in nonprofit organizations. They spent their last three months in Quito, Ecuador, working in a Catholic street ministry. During Mardi Gras weekend a number of volunteers and staff members, both Ecuadorians and Americans, rented a bus and traveled to the coast to spend a couple of days relaxing on the beach.

Not surprisingly, the beach was packed with people. Catherine decided to go for a swim to escape the crowds and enjoy some solitude. Swimming in deep water far from shore, she noticed a speed boat fast approaching her. The driver did not appear to see her. She yelled and waved as best she could, but to no avail. The boat continued on course. She finally decided to dive head first to get out of the way. She waited a split second too long. The prop caught her on her lower back. She knew immediately that she had been cut badly and would probably drown. Two thoughts immediately came to her mind, both quintessentially Catherine. The first expressed a sense of surprise, as if the accident were an irritating interruption. *I wasn't planning to die this young,* she said to herself. The second was a pleasant thought, borne out of the experience of losing her mother. *I get to see my mom!*

As it turned out, her first thought was the more accurate. Two young Ecuadorians witnessed the accident from shore and frantically swam to her, reaching her in just enough time. Once on shore, she was rushed to a medical tent where an EMT began to work on her. He stopped the bleeding, cleaned out the gaping wounds and stitched her up as best he could. However nauseated, Bethany stood by her through the entire ordeal, holding her hand, praying for her and singing hymns to her. Another friend secured transportation back to Quito; the trip took roughly seven hours, much of it over gravel roads. Once in Quito, they took her to a missionary hospital where a plastic surgeon removed the provisional stitches, cleaned out the wounds and then sewed her back up with over a hundred stitches.

Over the next week Catherine discovered what it means to belong to the worldwide church. As word spread, people in the United States contacted Christian friends in Quito, who began to visit and help her. A retired missionary doctor, for example, stopped in to see her every day and took personal responsibility for her care. People sent her letters, emails, flowers and gifts. Though complete strangers, they treated her like a dear friend and showered her with attention and affection. She felt like a celebrity. Over the course of the next month she kept telling me about it. "I just can't believe it, Dad. Those people loved me for no other reason than that I needed to be loved."

"It's the church," I responded. I told her that when the church is functioning at its best, there is simply no community on earth that can rival it. But when the church is functioning at its worst, there is no community on earth that can do as much damage. History itself proves the point. The church has served untold millions, as is evidenced by the number of churches, hospitals, orphanages, schools and relief agencies that Christians have founded and operated. But the church has brutalized untold millions, too, as the medieval inquisition and the religious wars of the seventeenth century demonstrate.

Catherine's case was admittedly unique. She was back on her feet in two days; she was released from the hospital in five days; she returned to the ministry one week later. Not everyone is as easy to love and care for as Catherine; not everyone bounces back as quickly; not everyone has a personality as winsome as hers and friends as loyal as hers. Obviously her case was special. Still, how Christians responded to Catherine's crisis shows what the church is capable of doing. If only the church rose to the occasion more often!

After the crisis had passed, I began to think about the many people I know whose needs are not so obvious and convenient, whose personalities are not so attractive, whose friends are not so compassionate. Catherine's experience proved the church's potential; it also reminded me of how seldom the church actually performs up to that potential. In truth I hear more horror stories about the church than heroic stories. I hear about immorality, disagreements, gossip, judgment, even hatred, all within the church. Christians complain about the preacher, the nursery, the youth program and the music. They say that the parking lot is too small, the organ too loud, the carpet too dirty, the worship too liturgical (or contemporary), the sermons too boring, the theology too conservative (or liberal), the decorations too cheap, the members too unfriendly. They are often right too. I have heard my fair share of bad sermons and visited many churches that treated me as if I were a leper. Christians do not always—in fact, do not often—behave as their faith demands.

THE CHARGE TO THE CHURCH

The church is a far cry from what God intended. If anything, the New Testament teaches that the church ought to be the exact opposite of what we usually see and experience. It is supposed to be Christ's dynamic presence in the world, his body on earth. The church is called to embody and imitate the very life of Jesus. Christians believe that Jesus Christ was God in human flesh. He came to earth to show us exactly who God is and what God was willing to do to deal with the problem of sin, which he accomplished through his death and resurrection. His mission completed, he ascended into heaven and returned to his father.

But his ministry of proclamation and service had just begun. He commissioned his disciples to continue that work. "All authority in heaven and on earth has been given to me," he told them. "Go therefore and make disciples of all nations, baptizing them in the name of the Father and of the Son and of the Holy Spirit, and teaching them to obey everything that I have commanded you. And remember, I am with you always, to the end of the age" (Matthew 28:18-20). This commission was—and still is—a formidable task. During his earthly lifetime Jesus' scope of influence

The church is called to embody and imitate the very life of Jesus.

was surprisingly limited. He conducted his public ministry for a mere three years; he confined his travels to Palestine; he preached to very few people and convinced even less. At his ascension he could number only 120 serious followers. Yet he commanded those followers to travel to every corner on the face of the globe and proclaim, in word and deed, the good news of the gospel. The book of Acts tells the story of how the church began to obey Jesus' command.

He charged the church to finish what he had started. The church is called to function as a body, as if it were a kind of incarnation of Christ in the world. "For just as the body is one and has many members, and all the members of the body, though many, are one body, so it is with Christ" (1 Corinthians 12:13). It is Paul's use of the word *Christ* in the passage that is so shocking, for the logic of his argument requires the word *church*, not *Christ*. But Paul is not following conventional logic here. Christ was the incarnation of God in the world; the church is the incarnation of Christ. Christ lived for only a short time and in a backwater place. His earthly impact was modest at best. It is the church that is charged with the responsibility to carry on where he left off. Unlike the earthly Christ, the church is not bound by time and space. It has existed for some two thousand years; it has developed some kind of witness in every major culture of the world.

THE SOURCE FOR THE CHURCH'S SUCCESS

Surprisingly, the church's success in this endeavor depends on only one thing: not great wealth, political power, sophisticated technology, superior organization, great preaching, public rallies, big buildings or creative programs, but the mutual love shared within the community of faith. The quality of relationships among Christians makes the church an effective witness for the gospel, for it creates the kind of community into which others are naturally drawn. "I give you a new commandment," Jesus told his disciples, "that you love one another. Just as I have loved you, you also should love one another. By this everyone will know that you are my disciples, if you have love for one another" (John 13:34-35). As one in community, God draws us into the perfect mutual love that exists within himself and allows us to participate in that love. He calls the church to become a community of mutual love in the world so that people will see and experience not only the love that believers have for each other but also the love that God has within himself.

Jesus himself is the source and center of that love. In his letter to the church in Ephesus Paul argued that Christ destroyed old animosities that existed in the ancient world between male and female, citizen and barbarian, slave and free, and especially Jew and Gentile. In Paul's day observant Jews considered themselves superior to Gentiles. They were the favored few, the recipients of the covenant, the law, the land, the temple and the promises. Gentiles were considered outsiders to this community, "without Christ, being aliens from the commonwealth of Israel, and strangers to the covenants of promise, having no hope and without God in the world." But all that changed when Jesus came. "But now in Christ Jesus you who once were far off have been brought near by the blood of Christ." Christ established peace and unity by breaking down "the dividing wall, that is, the hostility" between Jews and Gentiles. The cross of Christ exposed how the self-righteousness of Jewish religion had alienated Gentiles, and it showed that not even Jews, God's special people, had an advantage over others. Jews as well as Gentiles were sinners who needed grace and enemies of God who needed reconciliation. Conversely, Gentiles, too, could be children of God because of what Jesus had accomplished. Gentiles, therefore, were no longer strangers and sojourners but fellow "citizens with the saints and also members of the household of God."

Paul's pilgrimage of faith illustrates the point. As a devout Jew, he felt superior to Gentiles. He had reached the pinnacle of righteousness, far exceeding what the Gentiles could even hope to achieve. "If anyone else has reason to be confident in the flesh, I have more: circumcised on the eighth day, a member of the people of Israel, of the tribe of Benjamin, a Hebrew born of Hebrews; as to the law a Pharisee, as to zeal, a persecutor of the church, as to righteousness under the law, blameless." But his conversion on the Damascus road taught him that these religious accomplishments had kept him from Christ. "Yet whatever gain I had, these I have come to regard as loss because of Christ. More than that, I regard everything as loss because of the surpassing value of knowing Christ Jesus my Lord" (Philippians 3:4-8).

Paul's conversion transformed the way he viewed Gentiles. He had once thought that, as outsiders to Israel, Gentiles were simply a lower class of people. He saw Jesus as no better, regarding him as a renegade Jew, a law breaker and a menace to Jewish society. But when Paul discovered who Jesus really was, which occurred on the Damascus road, he began to see the Gentiles in a new light too. What mattered was no longer cultural background or religious performance but knowledge of Jesus Christ as Savior and Lord. "From now on, therefore, we regard no one from a human point of view; even though we once knew Christ from a human point of view, we know him no longer in that way. So if anyone is in Christ, there is a new creation: everything old has passed away; see, everything has become new!" (2 Corinthians 5:16-17).

In his classic book *Life Together*, Dietrich Bonhoeffer suggests that Jesus Christ provides the only foundation upon which the church can be built. He turns sinners into saints, transforms enemies into friends and enables believers to love one another. "Christianity means community through Jesus Christ and in Jesus Christ. No Christian community is more or less than this.

. . . We belong to one another only through and in Jesus Christ." There can be no other basis of unity, for any other basis—ethnic, political, ideological, educational, economic—always ends up giving an advantage to one group over another. "Now Christians can live with one another in peace; they can love and serve one another; they can become one. But they can continue to do so only by way of Jesus Christ. Only in Jesus Christ are we one, only through him are we bound together. To eternity he remains the one Mediator." Political affiliation, musical preference, national identity and religious background have no role to play in the church. Whether we affiliate with the Republican Party or the Democratic Party, whether we prefer "traditional" music or "contemporary" music, whether we admire Martin Luther King Jr. or Ronald Reagan is all of secondary importance. It is Jesus Christ alone who creates unity, who binds believers

> *Only Jesus Christ can and will make the church what God intends it to be, a community of belonging, a loving home, a foretaste of heaven.*

together, and who reconciles sinners to himself and to each other. Jesus draws all believers together in him. Echoing the apostle Paul, Bonhoeffer concludes, "The more genuine and the deeper our community becomes, the more will everything else between us recede, the more clearly and purely will Jesus Christ and his work become the one and only thing that is vital between us. We have one another only through Christ, but through Christ we do have one another, wholly, and for all eternity." Only Jesus Christ can and will make the church what God intends it to be, a community of belonging, a loving home, a foretaste of heaven.

LEARNING TO LOVE

Jesus Christ loved the church into existence. His sacrificial death on the cross brought it into being, welcoming into one fold centurion, Pharisee, Samaritan and prostitute. He calls the church to be united in love. Rarely, however, do we actually see the church function that way. How can we help the church, as loveless as it is, become the loving community Jesus called into being through his death and resurrection?

The New Testament provides detailed instructions. The apostle Paul uses the metaphor of joints and ligaments to emphasize the necessity of nurturing healthy relationships in the church. Joints and ligaments keep the limbs of the human body connected so that the body can function properly. If joints and ligaments are healthy, then the body can do productive work. If they are not, then the body stops working altogether, as any person who has problems with his or her joints or ligaments will testify. The New Testament issues a series of commands to show us how to develop these healthy relationships. Called "mutuality commands" because they use the phrase "one another," these commands translate love into action, mitigate the tensions that inevitably surface among Christians, and mollify the differences among believers so that, instead of suspicion, conflict and division the church models trust, harmony and unity. They enable the church to become a community of love.

The easiest way to deal with differences and disagreements is to caricature, ridicule or dismiss our opponents. I work in an academic setting, and I am appalled by the behavior of many intellectuals who are supposed to excel at good judgment and rational discourse. More often than not ideology trumps fairness, slander overrides teachableness. Thus anyone who questions the morality of homosexuality is labeled "homophobic," anyone who raises questions about affirmative action is called a "racist," and anyone who appeals to the authority of Scripture is branded a "fundamentalist." Conversely, anyone who leans to the left is dismissed as a "liberal" or "feminist" or "radical." It is no different in the church. That differences and disagreement occur is normal and healthy. How we respond tests whether or not we are willing to love.

Mutuality will never erase the differences among Christians. Nor should it. But it will enable Christians to maintain healthy relationships and practice sacrificial love. It all comes down to how much we value relationships and how much we want to learn how to love. The integrity and witness of the church is at stake. If a healthy church is the goal, then the mutuality commands are the means to get us there. In each of the following chapters I will focus on one mutuality command, explaining its background, meaning and application. As we shall see, some of the commands—"welcome one another," for example—lay a sturdy foundation for healthy relationships in the church. Others—"encourage one another"—enable us to maintain those relationships over a long period of time; still others—"comfort one another"—help us to get people through crises; finally, a few—"admonish one another"—show us how to reach and restore wayward brothers and sisters in Christ.

I look back on my daughter's accident in Quito. She has long since recovered. In fact, she did not stay home long after she returned with Bethany from her trip to Central and South America. Six months later she took a job in Bogota, Colombia, teaching language arts in a bilingual school. Over the years she has been the recipient of a great deal of love; she was one of the fortunate people who has seen the church function at its best, not only in Quito but through most of her life. She wants to return the favor, especially to people in need. She understands the value of relationships, the beauty and power of love, the potential the church has to embody that love to the world.

The mutuality commands tell us how to put love into action. I invite you to join me as we explore these commands and then try to obey them. It could be that we will be able to help the church become what Jesus designed it to be, his body on earth, an incarnation of his sacrificial love, a witness to the perfect love that exists within the very being of God as Father, Son and Holy Spirit.

2

Welcome One Another

*Welcome one another, therefore, just as Christ
has welcomed you, for the glory of God.*

ROMANS 15:7

The power we have to embrace or to reject people is almost unlimited.

In the late nineteenth century Frederick Treveds, a London physician, spotted the picture of a hideously deformed creature on the marquee of a "freak" exhibition and decided to take a closer look at "the Elephant Man." Winding through a dark, dusty passageway, he finally entered a large room. A showman barked at the freak to stand up and uncover himself. Treves recorded what followed:

> The most striking feature about him was his enormous and misshapened head. From the brow there projected a huge bony mass like a loaf, while from the back of the head there hung a bag of spongy, fungous-looking skin, the surface of which was comparable to brown cauliflower. On the top of the skull were a few long hairs. The osseous growth of the forehead almost occluded one eye. The circumference of the head was no less than that of the man's waist. From the upper jaw there projected another mass of bone. It protruded from the mouth like a pink stump, turning the upper lip inside out and making

of the mouth a mere slobbering aperture. . . . The nose was merely a lump of flesh, only recognizable as a nose from its position. The face was no more capable of expression than a block of gnarled wood.

Treves was so fascinated that he brought the man to the hospital and quartered him there. Quite sure the man was an imbecile, Treves was shocked one day to discover that his specimen was a real human being, intelligent, sensitive and kind. He also had a name, John Merrick. Merrick had learned to read and write before his mother abandoned him at the age of five. From that point on his life had been a succession of experiences as horrible as the appearance of his body. Though treated like an animal, he had nevertheless preserved vestiges of humanity deep within himself. Treves wrote:

> His troubles had ennobled him. He showed himself to be a gentle, affectionate and lovable creature, as amiable as a happy woman, free from any trace of cynicism or resentment, without a grievance and without an unkind word for anyone. I have never heard him complain. I have never heard him deplore his ruined life or resent the treatment he had received at the hands of callous keepers. His journey through life had been uphill all the way, and now, when the night was blackest and the way most steep, he had found himself, as it were, in a friendly inn, bright with light and warm with welcome. His gratitude to those about him was pathetic in its sincerity and eloquent in the childlike simplicity with which it was expressed.

Treves and Merrick soon became good friends, and Merrick began to recover his health and enjoy the security of living in the hospital environment. Still, Treves noticed that something seemed to have a hold on Merrick, some hidden fear or painful memory. Treves considered what he could do to shake Merrick loose from his bondage. He finally decided to invite Merrick to visit a widow friend as the first step toward introducing him to a wider circle of people. The idea was risky, for most people, especially women, recoiled from

Merrick in horror and disgust. But when Treves introduced him to his friend, she graciously wished Merrick a good morning, smiled at him warmly and took his hand in hers. As Merrick let go of her hand, he rested his huge head on his knees and began to sob. Treves discovered the reason later:

> He told me afterwards that this was the first woman who had ever smiled at him, and the first woman, in the whole of his life, who had shaken hands with him. From this day the transformation of Merrick commenced and he began to change, little by little, from a hunted thing into a man.

I don't know many people like John Merrick, real freaks who have had to endure deformity, pain and rejection for a lifetime. Still, I know many people who *feel* like John Merrick at least some of the time. Like Merrick, they are longing and waiting for the same acceptance that one dear widow extended to Merrick. That, in essence, is what it means to "welcome one another."

EMBRACE WITH LOVE

The apostle Paul explored the significance of this mutuality command in his letter to the church in Rome. Though he had never visited the church, he knew that a self-appointed group of "strong" or mature Christians had imposed their convictions concerning diet on "weak" or immature—and most likely new—Christians, thus forcing them to violate their conscience by eating meat that had been offered as a sacrifice to pagan gods. Paul acknowledged that these strong Christians were right, at least concerning diet. Christians were in fact free to eat what they wanted, even meat that had been offered as a sacrifice to pagan gods. But the weak Christians in Rome were not able to shake their scruples, however foolish and unnecessary, and thus believed that they were wrong to eat such meat. Paul argued, however, that the controversy was not simply—or primarily—about food; it was really about love. "If your brother or sister is being injured by what you eat, you are no longer walking in love" (Romans 14:15). If the strong Christians followed one law, it was to be the law of love. Paul exhorted them to "welcome one another in love," just as Christ had welcomed them. As the ministry of Christ shows, to welcome requires us to embrace people *as they are,* whether strong or weak, educated or ignorant, right or wrong, saint or sinner.

INITIATIVE AND GENEROSITY

The New Testament uses the term "greet" to make the same point. It conveyed a sense of warm acceptance and genuine interest, going far beyond our superficial "hello." It was a way of saying, "I'm glad you're alive; I'm glad I know you; I'm glad we're friends."

The Gospels give the term their own distinctive stamp. Jesus poured special meaning into it, conforming the idea to his unique calling and ministry. He presented two negative examples to make his point, using the Pharisees as the first example of what *not* to do.

> But woe to you Pharisees! For you tithe mint and rue and herbs of all kinds, and neglect justice and the love of God; it is these you ought to have practiced, without neglecting the others. Woe to you Pharisees! For you love to have the seat of honor in the synagogues and to be greeted with respect in the marketplaces. Woe to you! For you are like unmarked graves, and people walk over them without realizing it. (Luke 11:42-44)

The Pharisees regularly dressed up in their religious garb and paraded through the marketplaces, where they expected to be saluted and admired by the common people. Jesus warned his disciples not to behave so pretentiously and arrogantly. They were not to expect a greeting from others; they were to give a greeting first. They were to be "there you are" kind of people rather than "here I am" kind of people and thus to behave like Jesus, who paid special attention to the people everybody else overlooked and who did not use his popularity, prestige or greatness to separate himself from the common folk. He was an initiator in relationships. He acted immediately to welcome whoever crossed his path.

Jesus cited the Gentiles as the second negative example.

> You have heard that it was said, "You shall love your neighbor and hate
> your enemy." But I say to you, Love your enemies and pray for those
> who persecute you, so that you may be children of your Father in
> heaven; for he makes his sun rise on the evil and on the good, and
> sends rain on the righteous and on the unrighteous. For if you love
> those who love you, what reward do you have? Do not even the tax
> collectors do the same? And if you greet only your brothers and sisters,
> what more are you doing than others? Do not even the Gentiles do the
> same? Be perfect, therefore, as your heavenly Father is perfect. (Mat-
> thew 5:43-48)

Jesus acknowledged that the Gentiles were friendly, but only to their own
kind. They were nice to the people who were nice in return. Such strict rec-
iprocity did not require true faith or demonstrate genuine love. There was
no risk in it at all. Jesus said that his disciples had to do better by greeting
those who were not part of their natural circle of friends. That included the
foreigner, the newcomer, the oddball and even the enemy. Jesus required
that his disciples treat people as if they really counted for something, which
of course they do, at least in the eyes of God.

Jesus commanded his disciples, therefore, to be generous with their
greetings. They were not to let differences in color, personality, interest,
background, social status, economic level and religious conviction tempt
them to show favorites in the family of God, nor to let an expectation of re-
payment lead them to welcome into their lives only those who would return
the favor. Jesus warned against such base motives and actions.

> When you give a luncheon or a dinner, do not invite your friends or
> your brothers or your relatives or rich neighbors, in case they may in-
> vite you in return, and you would be repaid. But when you give a ban-
> quet, invite the poor, the crippled, the lame, and the blind, And you
> will be blessed, because they cannot repay you. (Luke 14:12-14)

As James exhorted, believers should avoid any display (or even suggestion) of partiality. We are to treat the poor no differently than we treat the rich, women no differently than men, children no differently than adults, the marginal no differently than the powerful. Jesus set a worthy example, going out of his way to include women, lepers, children, the poor and common folk in his circle of friends.

While the command to greet one another should affect all of our relationships, it's especially applicable within the body of Christ, where we are prone to draw sharp doctrinal and moral boundaries out of concern for the faith. To welcome and greet people implies that, no matter who they are and what they believe, we will always strive to embrace fellow believers in love and thus not erect barriers—cultural, religious, economic, political—that create distance, suspicion and misunderstanding. Such a spirit of acceptance is particularly important when we first meet people, when initiative and generosity create a climate for future growth.

This mutuality command played a dominant role in the apostle Paul's life. He encouraged others to obey it, and he practiced it himself. In virtually every one of his letters Paul extended his greetings to fellow believers or relayed greetings from others. "The churches of Asia send greetings. Aquila and Prisca, together with the church in their house, greet you warmly in the Lord" (1 Corinthians 16:19). Through his many years of ministry Paul established an extensive network of relationships and enlarged that network through his greetings. The popular view of Paul is of a stern and judgmental man. But the final chapters of many of his letters reveal another—and probably more accurate—side of the apostle. He was a man who knew how to welcome, include and affirm.

Nowhere is this more evident than in the final chapter of Romans, where Paul shows us how powerful and positive the act of greeting can be. He provides a model, which we will look at more closely: We extend greetings by acknowledging people, by commending accomplishments, by expressing affection and by conferring a blessing.

ACKNOWLEDGING PEOPLE

Ethel, a single parent, had three children. Recently divorced, Ethel decided to move to a bigger city where she landed a good job at a large corporation. She was welcomed at her place of employment and eventually began to make friends. The same could not be said, however, of her life outside of work. She bought a house in a new suburban subdivision and hoped that she and the children would develop friendships there. But her neighbors did not seem interested. They were either too busy or too private to be neighborly.

Fortunately, Ethel also had the church. Her past experience of church life had been positive; she had always been a church insider up to this point. Still, this was the first time she'd had to find a new church, and she was nervous. Over the next year she learned what it was like to hunt for a parking place and a nursery, to be seated in the sanctuary while she was sized up by the regulars, to practice new ways of worshiping, to meet people after the service who didn't know what to say once they learned her name, asked where her husband was and inquired about the reasons for her move. Sometimes she was completely ignored, often in large churches where the members probably didn't know each other well enough to realize she was a visitor. In church after church she met many people but made few friends, and sometimes she didn't meet anyone at all.

Ethel finally found a church home, but not before she went through the agony of being an outsider. Through this experience she learned what many Christians already know, that churches often make it difficult for newcomers to feel welcomed and wanted.

The ability to acknowledge and accept people is a rare gift that few of us possess and all of us need. Most of us forget names once we hear them and overlook people once we meet them. We pay attention to the people we already know, or to the ones we want to know. The few powerful, popular, witty, rich and successful people attract the biggest following, even at church. The quiet, elderly, odd, ordinary and undesirable are often left alone, like the lepers of Jesus' day.

I am impressed by the masterful way Paul extended greetings to the Romans in chapter 16. He referred to many people by name, some of whom he had never met in person but knew only through mutual friends. Paul remembered special details about these individuals. He remembered that Epaenetus was "the first convert in Asia," that Andronicus and Junias were "in Christ" before Paul was and were respected by the other apostles, that Prisca and Aquila had "risked their necks" for him. Also, scholars have discovered that half of the names of the people Paul greeted in Romans 16 were those of slaves and women, two groups that had little social power and respect. Unlike many of us, Paul did not calculate who were the right people to know. "From now on, therefore, we regard no one from a human point of view. . . . If

> *The ability to acknowledge and accept people is a rare gift that few of us possess and all of us need.*

anyone is in Christ, there is a new creation: everything old has passed away; see, everything has become new!" (2 Corinthians 5:16-17).

Christian groups often become exclusive over time, however sincere their desire to welcome newcomers and outsiders. Churches become ingrown; colleges become closed to new influences and fresh perspectives; committees become stifled by "good old boys" who make it almost impossible for new people to get involved. It's easy for us to keep "our people" in power and, consequently, to alienate new people who have not had the time or interest to join our party or take up our cause. Moreover, it's natural to concentrate on our current friendships—over coffee on Sunday mornings, at the office during the week—usually at the expense of new ones. We find it difficult and inconvenient to welcome people who don't speak our language, occupy our social and economic level, share our interests or hold our religious convictions. It takes effort to include them in our social networks and, frankly, many of us don't have the time, energy or interest.

The size of a group doesn't seem to matter. I have visited small churches that made me feel I had offended them by coming, and I have visited large churches that made me feel as if I were the only visitor they had seen in a year.

Lynda and I once visited a large church near Minneapolis. We had read about the church's beautiful architecture, so we arrived early enough to study the building and planned to leave immediately after the service. Our plans were thwarted, however, by the friendliness of the people. They would not let us go! After worship we were greeted by dozens of people who, much to our surprise, identified us as visitors even though there were fifteen hundred people at the church. They learned our names, engaged us in conversation, discovered our interests and introduced us to people with similar interests. Three times we were invited to someone's home for dinner. We chatted with people in the narthex for an hour before we could break away. We discovered later that the church has developed a special ministry of welcoming; certain people see their calling as folding newcomers into the fellowship of the church. Is it any wonder that we wanted to return? We only regretted not living closer to Minneapolis.

COMMENDING ACCOMPLISHMENTS

Another way to greet brothers and sisters in Christ is to commend their accomplishments and share with others the service they have rendered to God. Again, Paul was a master at this. He began his litany of greetings at the end of his letter to the Romans by singling out Phoebe, the carrier of the letter, for special praise.

> I commend to you our sister Phoebe, a deacon of the church at Cenchreae, so that you may welcome her in the Lord as is fitting for the saints, and help her in whatever she may require from you, for she has been a benefactor of many and of myself as well. (Romans 16:1-2)

The terms Paul used to describe Phoebe carried special weight: sister, deacon, benefactor. After honoring this worthy woman, he charged the believers in Rome to receive and assist her so she would be able to execute her responsibilities speedily.

Paul accomplished two purposes in this short introduction. First, he made Phoebe feel important and useful. Paul was practicing then what behavioral science has now proven: people respond best when they are praised, not when they are criticized. Second, he created a sense of mutual respect and obligation between Phoebe and the Roman Christians. They had high admiration for each other before they ever met because Paul had prepared the way.

Paul reminds us of something we already know through personal, and often painful, experience. We wield the power to enhance or destroy people's reputation simply by how we talk about them. The Bible is brutally direct in its warnings regarding the tongue (Luke 12:1-3; Matthew 12:36; James 3:2-12; Ephesians 4:29). Too often we make up our mind about people before meeting them because we listen to—and sometimes seek out—the "informed" opinions of others. We don't give people a chance to show us who they really are, especially if that impression differs from their previous reputation.

Sadly, this practice is standard fare in the body of Christ. "Shawn is an obnoxious and difficult student," a second-grade teacher at a Christian school says to fellow teachers in the teacher's lounge, giving Shawn a reputation that will stalk him the rest of his years in elementary school. "She's competent, all right, but her ambition and thirst for power are just too much for me," a supervisor in a Christian organization says to his boss about Jane, though that supervisor has never addressed the issue in her evaluation. "He's rigid, narrow and uptight," a pastor on the staff of a large church whispers about the senior pastor.

What is the difference between spiritual discipline and fanatical devotion? Between assertiveness and aggressiveness? Between flexibility and irresponsibility? Between attention to detail and fastidiousness? The difference often lies in what we choose to see. We extend godly greetings in the body of Christ when we commend the best side of our brothers and sisters without overlooking their weaknesses. Surely Phoebe wasn't perfect. Neither was Paul stupid and naive. He simply decided to share a good report about her, though he could have done otherwise. He considered it his responsibility to accent the positive, especially when talking about her in public.

This manner of greeting demands a special effort when we deal with our Christian opponents. We are inevitably tempted to recruit people or be recruited to the "right" side in an ideological battle. Pastors, professors and lay people are often encouraged to join a side or to take up a cause when they first arrive at a church, college or other Christian institution. "You could really enhance the evangelical witness at a time when we need to counteract the influence of _____." Or "Your commitment to social justice will provide a useful corrective to people like _____, who are too narrow and privatistic in their faith." These newcomers are not allowed to make up their own mind about people. The stakes are too high! Instead, they have to be given the right angle on things. They have to be informed about the *real* problems dogging the community. They have to be recruited to join a party of people whose minds are already made up.

> *We extend godly greetings when we commend the best side of our brothers and sisters.*

The apostle Paul did not always share good reports about people. He was on occasion direct and forceful in denunciating those he considered threats to the faith. "By rejecting conscience, certain persons have suffered shipwreck in the faith; among them are Hymenaeus and Alexander, whom I have turned over to Satan, so that they may learn not to blaspheme" (1 Timothy 1:19-20). But this was the exception. If anything, Paul erred on the side of generosity, unless the integrity of the gospel was at stake.

EXPRESSING AFFECTION

A good friend of mine who was raised in white, middle-class culture spent a year working as an intern in an inner-city church. In his religious background, the greeting during worship lasted about twenty seconds and consisted of a few handshakes and subdued hellos. So during his first Sunday in this new setting, he rose to smile politely and shake a few hands. He quickly learned that such was not the custom at this church. He was hugged by one person after another, all of whom welcomed him to their church. He sat down five minutes later to catch his breath, only to discover that he was the only one sitting down. The greeting took another ten minutes before formal worship resumed. Such was his introduction to the holy kiss in an African American church.

"Greet one another with a holy kiss," Paul says in Romans 16:16. This holy kiss was practiced regularly in the apostolic church, and by the second century was included in the communion liturgy. Even today many churches "pass the peace"—usually a handshake or a hug—as a way of turning believers' attention to one another even during formal worship.

Modern culture has perverted our understanding of sexuality—we don't know how to express filial love physically. We might be conscious of our bodies, but we don't feel comfortable using them in relationships except for erotic purposes. We thus treat people as if they were nothing but a body or, conversely, as if they had no body at all. The Christian "holy kiss" reminds us that our greetings should convey affection and that our bodies should be used to show love instead of lust.

Again, Paul expressed such affection in word as well as action. Many of his letters communicate an unmistakable tone of real love. For example, to the Philippians he wrote:

> It is right for me to think this way about all of you, because I hold you in my heart, for all of you share in God's grace with me, both in my imprisonment and in the defense and confirmation of the gospel. For God is my witness, how I long for all of you with the compassion of Christ Jesus. (Philippians 1:7-8)

The conclusion to his letter to the Romans contains phrase after phrase that communicates affection. He calls Ampliatus and many others his "beloved in the Lord." He calls Andronicus and Junias his "relatives" and Urbanus his "co-worker in Christ." Paul said verbally what he no doubt demonstrated physically. He greeted his fellow Christians with a holy kiss.

Today, we must translate the concept of the holy kiss into expressions more suitable to our time and place. But the intent should remain the same. A Presbyterian handshake has just as much power to communicate affection as a Pentecostal hug or Middle Eastern kiss. It can be kind and gracious or cold and lifeless; likewise, a hug can be warm and hearty or calculating and suggestive. At this point we must sound the depths of our hearts. Do we really want to embrace one another in love? Are we willing to use our total selves to show such love? Are we impartial in the way we embrace our brothers and sisters?

Some people stand in special need of holy affection. These are the "untouchables" of our culture. Jesus embraced the untouchables of his day: lepers, children, prostitutes, tax collectors. We have our own to love: the elderly, the poor, the sick and the ugly. I know widows who long for the tender touches their spouses once gave. I know homely people who want to be treated as something other than a displeasing face or figure. I know terminally ill people who crave to have someone break through the barrier of their illness. I met a young woman years ago who told me that she had never, since entering junior high, been touched by a man. She was starved for love and affection. We may rightly fear giving other people "the wrong impression" and recoil from "leading people on." These concerns, however, should not keep us from showing love. We must respect limits but not withhold expressing affection. Untouchables have a special need for demonstrations of genuine caring.

CONFERRING A BLESSING

Our greeting must include something else: the divine blessing. It should confer a spiritual benediction on both the people we know and the people we meet for the first time.

Every night before my wife retired to bed she slipped into the rooms of our four children and prayed for them, laying her hands gently on their heads. She was bestowing on them God's blessing. I carried on that custom from the time of her death until my kids began to stay up later than I did. Our children need it desperately. But who doesn't?

Paul usually included a benediction of grace and peace in his letters. "The God of peace be with all of you. Amen" (Romans 15:33). "The grace of the Lord Jesus be with you. My love be with all of you in Christ Jesus. Amen" (1 Corinthians 16:23-24). "The grace of our Lord Jesus Christ be with your spirit, brothers and sisters. Amen" (Galatians 6:18). Here our greetings convey both human love and divine favor. Paul was not merely talking about a blessing; he was imparting it.

In doing so, Paul was drawing on a rich Old Testament tradition. The "blessing" was standard practice among the people of God from the very beginning. Fathers pronounced a blessing on their children, a leader on the people. The blessing was given through prophetic utterance or the change of a name. Such a blessing communicated God's favor. The loss of blessing was considered a terrible curse, as we learn from Esau, who wept bitterly when his father decided to let the blessing on Jacob remain, even though he had received it under false pretense.

Esau's cry—"O Father, bless me!"—has echoed through the centuries in the hearts of those who have never received a greeting that carries the blessing of God. Children, parents, spouses, lovers, colleagues and friends want to know that our love for them reflects the love of God, that our love for them channels the love of God. People want to know that God's favor rests on them. They depend on us, at least in part, to receive that blessing.

Our Christian enemies need that blessing too. I am not proposing that we ignore or dismiss tensions in the church today, but I am suggesting that we mitigate them by praying the favor of God on our Christian opponents whenever we meet them, whether in cordial or adversarial situations. They belong to God, as we do; they believe in God, as we do; they stand in need of God, as we do. The substance of our disagreements might not change, but the spirit of the relationship often will if in our greetings we bestow God's blessing. We need to remind our opponents that though we differ with them in theology or practice, we still regard them as Christian brethren.

The good news of the gospel is that God has welcomed us in Christ Jesus. Jesus told us so in the parable of the prodigal son, which is really about a longing and loving father. Recognizing that he had to let his rebellious son go, the father waited anxiously for some sign of his return. When he finally spotted him at a distance, the father rushed out to greet his son, welcomed him home with a hug, clothed him with a robe, put a ring on his finger and gave him shoes to wear. Then he killed a fatted calf and threw a party. Jesus said that that father is like God, who embraces us in love, however prodigal we are, and welcomes us into his family, however undeserving we are. He charges us to do the same for our Christian brothers and sisters.

3

Be Subject
to One Another

"Be subject to one another out of reverence for Christ."

EPHESIANS 5:21

Lynda and I used to watch old movies on public television. It gave us a chance to take in classic entertainment and to enjoy the performances of great actors and actresses, many of whom have long since died. Over the years we saw several movies starring Fred Astaire, who appeared in dozens of films over a span of four decades. We never tired of his films, despite the predictable plots and mediocre acting. It was Astaire's dancing that astonished us. He was a master on the dance floor, the embodiment of grace, effortlessness and sophistication. He looked at home in tails and a top hat.

After his death Ginger Rogers, Astaire's famous dancing partner, was interviewed on *Nightline*. Ted Koppel invited her to reminisce about Astaire's career and her experience as his dancing partner. It was obvious that she relished the opportunity to reflect on their magical years together. He was so good, she said, that he never seemed to be leading and she following. The film clips proved her point. There was a fluidity between the two of them, a seamlessness, an elegance, as if two people were dancing as one.

DANCING IN A BROKEN WORLD

Astaire and Rogers manifested in dance what God wants all of us to experience in life. He intends human relationships to be healthy, harmonious and whole so that, regardless of the positions we occupy in the social order, we will not be aware of who is leading and who is following, who has the most power and who has the least. God wills that human relationships exhibit the same kind of seamlessness that Astaire and Rogers demonstrated on the dance floor.

Of course what God intends and what we experience are very different. It is often the case that instead of oneness we experience disunity, instead of wholeness, brokenness. In human society—which of course includes the church—we spend most of our time not dancing gracefully but tripping over each other's feet. Rarely do we find human relationships that do not have conflict and do not cause hurt. I work in an academic institution, and I witness conflicts so often that I marvel when I hear about normal, healthy relationships and departments. A friend recently reminded me that conflict can serve as a prelude to harmony. I agree with him too. But I wish I saw more examples of harmony to reassure me that he is indeed right.

Mutual subjection is God's way of nurturing harmony in a discordant world, unity in broken relationships, healing in a sick society and love in a divided church. It is applicable to imperfect people—like you and me—who belong to imperfect families, work imperfect jobs, participate in imperfect organizations, belong to imperfect churches and live in an imperfect world. It shows us how to function in communities that have tension and conflict running through them. It addresses people who are *not* married to the ideal spouse, who are *not* parents of ideal children, who are *not* members of ideal churches, and who do *not* have ideal jobs, colleagues and bosses. Mutual subjection takes the world as it is, not as we want or expect it to be. It requires us to surrender ourselves to God, discerning how we can do his will in circumstances that are less than ideal.

This is the one mutuality command that addresses life in the social order, which is a necessary reality. *All* of us belong to and play certain roles within society. For example, over the past few years I have functioned as a son, brother, father, professor, coach, chaplain, board member, volunteer, administrator, committee chair, citizen and leader. As a professor, I deal every day with students, colleagues, administrators and secretaries. As a church member, I interact regularly with pastors, elders, youth leaders, Sunday school teachers, committee members and the like. These roles are defined by the institutions to which I belong. Not every institution runs smoothly, not every person is pleasant to work with or does his or her job well, not every task is

Mutual subjection takes the world as it is, not as we want or expect it to be.

meaningful and fulfilling. Mutual subjection provides guidelines for how to function with good cheer and responsible behavior in a social order that does not always run smoothly.

ORDERING OUR UNDERSTANDING OF SUBJECTION

Of all the mutuality commands, this one is perhaps the most difficult to understand and obey because it runs so contrary to modern values. Americans insist on defending their personal rights and securing or maintaining their social privileges, which makes the idea of subjection both foreign to our thinking and offensive to our cultural sensibilities. It appears to reinforce the power of those who already have too much and to keep the powerless in a place of subordination. Marxists argue that the biblical notion of subjection is a classic illustration of how Christianity supports the unjust social order and prevents the powerless from recognizing their servile status, developing a sense of class-consciousness and overthrowing the party or people in power. They conclude that Christianity is inherently conservative and oppressive.

This suspicion of or hostility toward mutual subjection is partly the fault of the church, too, which has often distorted the biblical meaning of the command. Throughout the two millennia of the history of Christianity the church has applied this command almost exclusively to those who occupy traditionally subordinate positions in society—children, wives, slaves, laborers, citizens and ordinary church members—and has failed to apply it to those who hold traditionally dominant positions in society—fathers, husbands, masters, rulers and church leaders. This imbalanced perspective has often made the subordinate group feel inferior, as if they *belonged* in a servile position and should therefore accept it as God's will; it has also made the dominant group feel invincible and arrogant, as if they had an absolute right to power and the freedom to use it as they wish. Most Christians, therefore, will not obey this command happily and willingly—if at all—without a reasonable explanation of what it means and does not mean.

The Greek term provides the clarity we need. It combines two words, one that could be translated "under" and the other "order." To be subject to one another implies that we choose to *order* our lives *under* the circumstances, relationships and roles in which we find ourselves. The three English words that are used to translate the Greek term—"subject," "subordinate" and "submit"—which all begin with the same prefix, *sub-*, connote the same meaning as the Greek term. In essence, to be subject to one another implies that we acknowledge the necessity of social order, accept our place within it, and transform the social order through the power of radical obedience and sacrificial love.

Obviously the word itself *assumes* the reality of order, which God himself created for our own good. God established a certain kind of order even in creation. What God created on the first day provided the proper setting for the second; what God created on the second day set the stage for the third. And so it continued until the last day of creation, when God created living creatures, first animals and then human beings. The account in Genesis 1 reads like a symphony in six movements, describes the ordering of creation in a rhythmic way, and spells out the vast diversity and differentiation we see so plainly in the world around us, whether in nature or in society. God saw all that he created, and he pronounced it good.

Human beings add to this magnificent work by imposing their own kind of order on the world. We create works of art, launch new ventures, found institutions, build churches. We imitate God in these endeavors too. There is nothing inherently wrong with order. If anything, we could not live without it.

I usually do several weddings every summer, and I often meet with couples ahead of time to get them ready for marriage. In the course of our premarriage counseling sessions, we explore issues like family background, communication, conflict, expectations and finances. I always ask them if they have discussed how they will establish division of labor in the home. What, I ask, will the husband do? The wife? They usually respond that they will do *everything* together—shopping, cleaning, cooking and other details. Of course it never ends up that way. Over time the husband gravitates toward some chores, the wife toward others. They discover that it is simply impossible, to say nothing of inefficient, to do *everything* together.

But the world is fallen too, which affects the social order in the same way it affects the natural order. The good order of society has become perverted and distorted. We see evidence of this everywhere. Marriages end in divorce because husband and wife refuse to love and serve each other. Parents neglect or abuse their children, and children rebel against their parents. Employers use their position to advance their own interests, often at the expense of employees; subordinates undermine the authority of their employers by complaining and performing poorly. Churches, of course, are no different. Pastors fail to execute their responsibilities faithfully; they play favorites and preach lousy sermons and get defensive when criticized. Meanwhile, parishioners expect to be entertained, refuse to volunteer for jobs that need to get done and criticize without knowing all the facts. Institutions always suffer when people fail to fulfill the roles assigned to them and to do the jobs expected of them.

An article recently ran in *Newsweek* telling the story of a young man who brought a gun to school and shot and wounded several students and a teacher before he was apprehended. The article described the history of this troubled young man. As one teacher said, he kept "slipping through the cracks." His mother was addicted to drugs, her live-in boyfriends abused him, classmates picked on him, and teachers always tried to pass him off to someone else. Every social institution that could have helped to reverse his downward spiral failed to do its job. He will spend years behind bars for his foolish action. As one teacher concluded, he was a victim of a system that "does not work."

The social order is a part of God's created order, both necessary and good. It is also perverse, fallen and failing. That is true of *every* human institution—marriage and family, churches, businesses, sports, the arts, education, government. We can't live with these institutions, and we can't live without them. Mutual subjection is the biblical command that enables us to function in these fallen institutions without a spirit of resignation or rebellion. We accept our proper place in the social order, but we also strive to change the social order through the power of sacrificial love.

RADICAL AND RELEVANT

The biblical texts that teach mutual subjection (especially Ephesians 5:21–6:10) seem excessively conservative to us now, embodying a view of reality that seems more fitting for ancient society than for ours. We fail to realize how radical this command really was in Paul's day and, in fact, still is today. There are four features that set it apart as both radical and relevant.

First, the command is addressed to *everyone*. "Be subject to one another out of reverence for Christ." Addressed, as it was, to the entire church community, Paul's words would have shocked his ancient readers, for he was speaking both to master and to slave, to husband and to wife, to parents and to children.

Paul requires that those who occupy dominant positions in the social order be subject to their subordinates; they are to order their lives *under* the very people *over* whom they exercise authority. Husbands are to be subject to their wives, fathers to their children, masters to their slaves, leaders to their followers and pastors to their flocks. Paul also issues this command to the people who occupy subordinate positions in the social order, treating them as free moral agents. He commands them to be subject even though they already *are* subject, at least according to the social roles they occupy. Subjection is thus a choice. The command concerns more than position; it concerns *how we function* in that position. That we occupy a position of subordination is less important, according to Paul, than what we do with it to glorify God.

Second, how we obey this command depends upon the particular position we occupy within the social order. There is differentiation, based on the roles we have been assigned by God. Though the command is universal, the application is particular. Husbands are to love their wives as Christ loved the church, sacrificing their lives for them; wives are to respect and honor their husbands. Fathers are to instruct and discipline their children; children are to obey their parents. Masters are to be fair to their slaves; slaves are to serve their masters from the heart.

The greater responsibility, however, appears to be imposed on those who occupy dominant positions. Paul commands husbands, fathers, masters, leaders and pastors to imitate Christ, who gave his life for sinners, though he had every right to assert power over them. When Jesus was describing the kind of leader he wanted his disciples to be, he proclaimed, "You know that among the Gentiles those whom they recognize as their rulers lord it over them, and their great ones are tyrants over them. But it is not so among you; but whoever wishes to become great among you must be your servant, and whoever wishes to be first among you must be slave of all. For the Son of Man came not to be served but to serve, and to give his life as a ransom for many" (Mark 10:42-45).

Third, mutual subjection appears to correct the natural abuses that occur within the social order, though without abolishing the social order itself. Take, for example, the institution of the family. When addressing parents, Paul speaks only to fathers, not even bothering to mention mothers. Why the apparent oversight? It is probably because he didn't need to speak to mothers, for they usually fulfill their role naturally because of biological predisposition and social expectation. But fathers are another matter altogether. What comes naturally to them is producing children, not rearing children, which explains why the vast majority of single parents are women, not men. Fathers tend to avoid domestic responsibilities. If they do remain in the home, they tend to neglect or abuse children, which, as Paul states, "provokes" them to anger. Fathers must therefore *learn* to function as good parents. Paul commands them to become active fathers, to train and discipline their children, and to help them grow up well.

Paul commands children to obey their parents "in the Lord." The root for the Greek word *obey* is to "listen" and to "hear." The kind of obedience Paul has in mind, in short, is not slavish but thoughtful. Children should ask, "What do my parents really have in mind?" "What is their intent?" "What is their primary concern?" Wise children listen to their parents in that kind of careful, reflective way. Paul quotes the fifth commandment to support his injunction. It is the one commandment, he says, that is accompanied with a promise. If children obey their parents, the commandment reads, their days in the Promised Land will be long and prosperous. The quality of their adult life, in short, depends at least in part on the quality of their relationships with parents, especially when they were children. As a general rule, obedient children will do well in life, disobedient children will not, probably because obedient children are willing to learn life lessons from the very people— namely, parents—who know them the best and who care for them the most. The skills, character and convictions they need to do well in life are developed most easily and conveniently at home, even under difficult circumstances. If not, they will have to be developed later in life, often through painful experiences. In short, what happens in the home, however imperfect that home is, will play itself out in the rest of life.

I was widowed many years ago. At the time of my wife's death my children were eight, seven and two years old. They are all adults now, which means that for the majority of their years growing up I was their only living parent (though their mother, Lynda, did play an important role *in absentia*). At the time of their mother's death I can say in good conscience that I was an active father; but I was also an ambitious professional who wanted to make a big splash in the world of higher education. I soon realized that those ambitions had to be subordinated to my duties as a single father. I discovered that I had to be subject to the needs of my children, especially considering how traumatized they were. Just last night we celebrated my daughter's engagement. Her brothers were there, family friends, her fiancé's family. My daughter is a wonderful young woman, and she is marrying a good man. They are committed to serving Christ together. My sons have pledged themselves to live such a life too. The entire evening reminded me of the wisdom of my decision to try, however falteringly, to be subject to my children, making decisions and conducting my life as if they really do matter, which of course they do.

This same principle of "correction" applies to husbands and wives. Men are naturally coercive, especially with women. Paul therefore commands husbands to love their wives as Christ loved the church, and Peter reminds husbands that, in spite of the apparent inequality of men and women in the social order, they are "joint heirs" of the grace of God. There will be no hierarchy in heaven. Husbands are therefore to honor their wives and to care for them, especially when they are vulnerable. If they fail to do this, Peter writes, their prayers will go unanswered (1 Peter 3:7). But wives, who often hold subordinate positions in society, resort to other, subtler means to get their way, such as badgering and manipulating their husbands. So Peter enjoins wives to win their husbands to Christ through a gentle and quiet spirit, and he advises them to dress modestly, thus demonstrating that purity and goodness matter more than getting their way (1 Peter 3:1-6). Mutual subjection requires all parties in the social order to hold their natural inclinations in check by striving to serve the best interests of others.

Finally, all Christians are to be subject to one another "out of reverence for Christ" or "as to the Lord." Paul adds this qualification for two reasons. First, he wants to remind us that the Son of God himself became subject *to us*, sinners though we are, all for the sake of our salvation. Though he was "in the form of God," he "did not regard equality with God as something to be exploited, but emptied himself, taking the form of a slave, being born in human likeness. And being found in human form, he humbled himself and became obedient to the point of death—even death on a cross" (Philippians 2:6-8). Second, he wants to assure us that Jesus Christ is now Lord over all.

> Therefore God also highly exalted him
> and gave him the name
> that is above every name,
> so that at the name of Jesus
> every knee should bend,
> in heaven and on earth and under the earth,
> and every tongue should confess
> that Jesus Christ is Lord,
> to the glory of God the Father. (2:9-11)

Subjection puts our rights and privileges at risk, which, considering the values of modern society, might seem foolish. But our subjection is ultimately to Jesus Christ, not to a human being or to a human institution. Jesus himself will act on our behalf, defend our rights and accomplish his good purposes. As the story of Joseph keeps repeating, the Lord was "with Joseph" in the very circumstances that seemed to run contrary to everything we would naturally and rightly expect of God. Joseph practiced subjection; God used that subjection to advance his sovereign plan. And all ended well. Though others did great evil, God "worked it out for good," at least in part because Joseph trusted God and chose to obey him.

Jesus is Lord over all. We can therefore never use our circumstances, however undesirable, as an excuse *not* to be subject. A spirit of subjection demonstrates that we believe God is truly in control, even when he does not seem to be. God might choose in his providence to put us in difficult circumstances—for example, forcing us to work for an excessively demanding employer or to pass through a challenging phase of parenthood or to face a church feud—to purge us of pride and to prepare us for some greater purpose. I have observed this kind of situation time and time again. A woman endures a period of hardship in a particular job, only to find herself several years later in a position of responsibility for which that hardship prepared her. A pastor faces a problem at church that over time ushers the church into a period of dramatic growth. A parent struggles to manage tumult at home, which years later leads to a ministry to distraught parents. If handled wisely, such challenges can set the stage for good work in the future.

Subjection therefore requires us to trust in the sovereignty of God. If we insist on perfect people and circumstances *before* we become subject, then of course we will never learn subjection. We will be forever waiting for the world to be conformed to *our* wishes rather than allowing God to use the world, however imperfect, to conform us to *his* wishes. The world—that is, our spouses, parents, coworkers, coaches, teachers, bosses—needs to change, of course. That goes without saying. But we need to change too. God will use the world *as it is* to make us more like Christ.

A spirit of subjection demonstrates that we believe God is truly in control, even when he does not seem to be.

HARMONY IS POSSIBLE

It is possible to be subject even when we choose to disobey those in authority over us, provided we challenge their authority in a spirit of subjection, honoring the person and position, though not necessarily their policies. When Roman authorities ordered Peter and John to refrain from preaching the gospel, the two intrepid apostles refused, saying that they were obligated to obey God rather than human authorities. But they were willing to go to jail for it, too, thus upholding the social order even as they challenged it. Martin Luther King Jr. did something of the same thing when he practiced nonviolent resistance to challenge the injustice of segregation. As in the case of Peter and John, he went to jail, which reflected his dual commitment to justice *and* to the integrity of the social order. The validity of his protest was in fact heightened by his willingness to go to jail. Thus he disobeyed authority and honored authority at the same time. He chose to resist evil by doing good (Romans 12:12-17). Jesus provides the quintessential example here. Though he had every right as the Son of God to call on the angels of heaven to punish the Jewish Sanhedrin and Roman government, he remained subject to both institutions, which resulted in his death and our salvation.

On occasion I have had an experience in institutions in which I felt as if I were gliding across the dance floor as effortlessly as Astaire and Rogers. I worked for a number of years in an academic department that functioned as harmoniously as any I have ever seen. We enjoyed each other's company, celebrated each other's successes and collaborated on various projects. But the harmony did not last forever. Eventually problems surfaced that disrupted the harmony and damaged relationships. Our little club of intimate relationships had to be expanded to include others that did not fit in so easily. We started to stumble across the dance floor, stepping on each other's feet and, sometimes out of frustration, kicking each other in the shin. We are still trying to resolve the problems. It is surprising, considering the fallenness of humanity, that that harmony lasted as long as it did. I am confident the problems will be resolved. Mutual subjection will help solve them, too, for subjection allows God to be in control and to accomplish his perfect will through very imperfect people and institutions, often in ways we never could have imagined.

4

Forbear One Another

With all humility and gentleness, with patience,

bearing with one another in love.

Ephesians 4:2

Many years ago I ran across an article in the *Los Angeles Times*. It told the story of several members of a fraternity who decided it would be fun to kidnap one of the pledges and take him on a "ride" to the hills north of Los Angeles. They jumped their victim in the middle of the night, tied, gagged and blindfolded him, and dropped him off in a deserted area. Their victim, of course, had no idea where he was. Removing his blindfold, he wandered around for a while to get his bearings. The overcast sky made the night very dark. So dark, in fact, that he didn't see the edge of the cliff over which he stumbled, falling to his death. The article said the students who kidnapped him felt horrible; they had no idea their prank would end in such tragedy. Police officers decided not to press charges because the boys were guilty "only of stupidity."

I remember this chilling article because I too have a propensity for stupidity. If I had been one of those fraternity members I would have participated as eagerly as the others. My track record confirms it. I have often spoken foolishly, decided prematurely and behaved badly. Perhaps you have as well.

God knows all about our stupidity and bears with us in spite of it, ever loyal to us. He is good at forgiving, putting up with, looking past and loving us through it. God is forbearing toward us.

The Bible mentions the forbearance of God often. In Psalm 78, for example, the psalmist exalts God's patience and compassion toward the people of Israel.

> Their heart was not steadfast toward him;
> > they were not true to his covenant.
> Yet he, being compassionate,
> > forgave their iniquity,
> > and did not destroy them;
> often he restrained his anger,
> > and did not stir up all his wrath.
> He remembered that they were but flesh,
> > a wind that passes and does not come again. (Psalm 78:37-39)

The apostle Paul made God's forbearance a foundational principle of his theology. In his pivotal argument of Romans 3:21-26 he used Israel's disobedience to make a point about the character and plan of God. God sent Jesus to be the propitiation for sin, the supreme sacrifice that makes believers right with God. Jesus came in the fullness of time to accomplish this great work. But what happened before Christ came? Paul argued that in his "divine forbearance" God passed over former sins in anticipation of Christ's death on the cross. He looked ahead to what would someday happen, putting up with their sinfulness because Jesus would pay the penalty.

God was forbearing then, and he is now. He suspended final judgment then because Jesus was coming; he suspends judgment now because Jesus has already come. With the people of Israel, he looked ahead; with us he looks back. In both cases he looks to Jesus, whose triumph on the cross enables him to forbear. It should stagger us to consider how much God forbears. He bears with and loves us despite our smallness of mind, defensiveness, bad moods, obnoxious personalities, sour attitudes and petty concerns. He forbears like good parents who recognize that their immature children will someday become mature adults. Yes, he does discipline and forgive us when needed. But he also forbears when forgiveness is not necessary, when discipline is not appropriate, when only time and experience will do the trick.

We have benefited more than we know from God's forbearance. God calls us to imitate him in forbearing one another. He commands us to give each other the slack he's given us. Forbearance requires that we give people room—room to be who they are, to become who God intends, to contribute to the church and the world despite their imperfections.

> *Forbearance requires that we give people room— room to be who they are, to become who God intends.*

The word *forbear* itself is important. A biblical word, it requires more than just politeness, which, although preferable to rudeness, can still hide a disdainful, condescending attitude. To forbear also implies more than tolerance, which has become an obsession in modern culture. Tolerance can smack of relativism and compromise. Forbearance demands politeness and tolerance but also so much more.

Forbearance is what I consider one of the foundational reciprocal commands, as are welcoming and subjection. It demands consistency. Rarely will our brothers and sisters in Christ accept our comfort if they have not benefited from our forbearance first; rarely will they allow us to bear their burdens; rarely will they yield to our admonitions. Forbearance builds trust, and trust makes people more willing to let a relationship grow, even when it becomes painful. The long-term vulnerability, openness and strength of our relationships depend on faithful obedience to this command. Failure to obey it will jeopardize unity whenever misunderstanding, wrongdoing or conflict—inevitable in any relationship—arise.

But how far do we forbear? Do we forbear departures from orthodox theology? Many Christians I know would forbear denial of the virgin birth and the inerrancy of Scripture. Very few would forbear rejection of the bodily resurrection of Christ from the dead. Is this distinction legitimate? Is the resurrection more central theologically and historically than the virgin birth? How do we make such difficult decisions?

Should we forbear violations of biblical morality? If so, how far is too far? Most Christians in America protest little, if at all, when fellow believers are materialistic. Not so in the case of adultery or homosexuality, although even that's changing rapidly.

To what degree should we forbear obnoxious personality traits and character blind spots? I know some wives who have put up with irresponsible husbands for years, treating them as children. Are these wives patient and forbearing or weak and indulgent? Some pastors have endured immaturity in certain members of the congregation for their entire tenure of service. Are they compassionate and sensitive or cowardly and naive?

Learning to discern when and how much to forbear is a little like mastering the art of parenthood. It's difficult to determine when aberrant behavior should be overlooked and when it should be confronted.

ROOM TO BE

The essential meaning of the Greek word for "forbear" is "to bear with," "to give slack to." Forbearance requires that we give people room to be themselves, that we accept them without communicating a spirit of disapproval or judgment, and that we rejoice in them as God's special creation. It's a way of saying, "This is who you are and I'm glad for it."

The apostle Paul commands forbearance of us in Ephesians 4:2. In that same verse he mentions three character qualities that make forbearance possible: lowliness, meekness and patience (RSV). Surely meekness is necessary if we're going to give people room to be who they are. Meek people don't try to remake others into copies of themselves. They don't impose their will. They're not tyrannical, dominant, judgmental or bossy. Meek people let God be Lord of their own lives and the lives of other people too.

Paul charged Christians to refrain from passing judgment on each other in areas that don't matter much. He argued, for example, that it was not important whether a person ate or abstained from certain foods for religious reasons. Because the issue did not involve a major biblical prohibition, Paul encouraged believers to be forbearing.

> Welcome those who are weak in faith, but not for the purpose of quarreling over opinions. Some believe in eating anything, while the weak eat only vegetables. Those who eat must not despise those who abstain, and those who abstain must not pass judgment on those who eat; for God has welcomed them. Who are you to pass judgment on servants of another? It is before their own lord that they stand or fall. (Romans 14:1-4)

Paul applied one basic rule in these circumstances: "Let us therefore no longer pass judgment on one another, but resolve instead never to put a stumbling block or hindrance in the way of another" (Romans 14:13). He was aware that "strong" Christians (those whose consciences were formed by biblical principles, not religious scruples) would be tempted to persuade their weaker brethren to give up misguided convictions about food laws, religious calendars and the like. He charged these strong Christians to "bear with" weak Christians in beliefs and customs that ultimately had no spiritual value. "We who are strong ought to put up with the failings of the weak, and not to please ourselves. Each of us must please our neighbor for the good purpose of building up the neighbor" (Romans 15:1-2).

These principles still apply. Many issues that divide Christians and create an artificial standard in the church simply don't count for much. How Christians dress, eat, play, talk, worship, observe the church year, witness, serve people in need, think politically—these and other areas contain room for interpretation and expression. Not that we should cast all standards to the wind. Some standards do apply in dress, speech, worship, witness and the like. But these broad standards break out of the narrow boundaries in which we often force our brothers and sisters to live. Forbearance prevents us from using our preferences and ideologies as a means of controlling people who stand with us in essential beliefs but depart from us in application, expression and style. Forbearance gives people room.

Many issues that divide Christians and create an artificial standard in the church simply don't count for much.

Church music is an area where it's best to give a great deal of room. Trained church musicians are often galled by the sentimental slop that passes for Christian music today, and theologians are offended by the shallow and insipid lyrics in many contemporary Christian songs. Other people, musically untrained but still opinionated, are put off by high church music. As they say, there isn't much beat and swing to J. S. Bach. They want to feel the music, not simply think about it. Both sides have a point. I'm impressed by music directors who use both kinds of music. They try to honor *and* to challenge those who want nothing but a contemporary sound or those who want nothing but Bach. They know how to compromise without caving in and to give people room to have differing musical tastes without capitulating to either side. Churches with these kinds of directors have livelier and deeper worship because of it.

The command to forbear requires us somewhere along the line to make up our minds about our fellow Christians. We have to decide whether to accept them in spite of their weaknesses or reject them because of their weaknesses. I believe that most Christians are basically good people who have a few irritating habits, personality quirks or peculiar beliefs. We all know the self-appointed experts who have the right answer to every problem, the bossy volunteers who take charge when no one wants to follow, the incompetent leaders who make everyone feel anxious because they don't get any work done and the self-absorbed friends who never stop talking about their problems. These are the ones we are called to forbear.

Our fellow Christians will know it too, and sense the attitude we communicate, whether disapproval or delight. Forbearing people impart a spirit of love and create a healthy environment for relational growth. While we lived in

Chicago my oldest daughter had a wonderfully forbearing preschool teacher. She was not necessarily an early childhood education expert or an unusually creative or energetic teacher. But she was able to discern and value the basic personality of each child. Consequently she related to each child differently. She did not prefer the bright children over the slow ones, the coy ones over the assertive ones, the serious ones over the silly ones. In her eyes, every child was special. To this day, some years later, my daughter still considers her an important person in her life. Forbearance has that kind of power.

Still, forbearance is not easy. It requires grace because people can be obnoxious. I am sure that over the course of her career my daughter's preschool teacher had students who tested her to the limit, and beyond. Over a normal lifetime all of us will know people who make forbearance seem more difficult than martyrdom. My late wife, for example, was put off by people who were insensitive, arrogant and rude. I am bugged by people whose psychological nerve endings seem to extend ten inches beyond their fingertips. Without the grace of God our best intentions and efforts will fall short of God's command. We will be tempted to withhold the love of Christ from people who drive us crazy.

Forbearance also requires humor, because sometimes laughter is the best—and the only sane—way we can respond to people. We have to learn to say, "Yes, that person bugs me. But I sure don't know anyone like her." Not everything, of course, is funny. Some matters are deadly serious, and we must treat them that way. But other things are not quite so serious. Terrible church soloists who lost their sense of pitch years ago and overbearing personalities who make us want to hide whenever we see them approaching— too often we pronounce judgment rather than chuckle. I am convinced that forbearing Christians smile a lot.

I have a minister friend whose wife, Darlene, an accomplished singer, was invited to be the soloist at a wedding. When she asked who the organist was, the bride assured her that she was a "professional musician." That satisfied Darlene until she arrived at the wedding and discovered that the "professional musician" performed pop electronic organ music—the kind played at skating rinks. She played pop tunes for her prelude and waved to people as they were ushered into the sanctuary. When Darlene stood up to sing her first solo, the organist rolled a chord and tipped her hand toward Darlene, much as a ringmaster would introduce a circus act. Though embarrassed, Darlene managed to make it through the wedding. Her ego was not so large that she couldn't laugh about it afterward.

Finally, forbearance requires discernment, for we still have to make judgments. As I have mentioned, not everything is funny. Forbearance does not mean we ignore defects, weaknesses, immaturity and sin. Sometimes faithful church members insist on singing solos when they are simply not qualified to perform that service. Sometimes church members make foolish decisions that strain the need for tolerance to the breaking point. Sometimes peculiar behavior cannot be written off as idiosyncratic but must be called what it is—irresponsible and destructive. We need discernment to decide when forbearance must give way to exhortation or admonition.

Jesus is our model of forbearance. He gave his disciples lots of room to be themselves. Has it ever surprised you how seldom Jesus rebuked his disciples, considering how often he could have? Peter made great claims about himself and repeatedly fell short of those claims. James and John were heartlessly insensitive on more than one occasion. Yet Jesus continued to forbear. He knew that their puny faith would someday make them spiritual giants. What he did for them then he does for us now. He sees who we are and loves us anyway. He calls us to follow his example.

ROOM TO BECOME

People change, but not always for the better. It takes a keen eye to trace the trajectory in a person's life and discern whether changes are for the better or for the worse. Forbearance enables us to look for and affirm a basic pattern of growth in our brothers and sisters, and it forces us to remember that what people are becoming is as important as who they presently are. Yet change can be slow, painfully slow. Sometimes it seems that people will never get the point, never change, never grow up. Is there no limit to forbearance?

This question helps us understand why Paul urged believers to be patient, a quality that, like meekness, helps us exercise forbearance. Patience is necessary if we're going to give people the time and space to mature in faith, knowledge and obedience—to become a better version of themselves. Such patience is a fruit of the Spirit, a gift that God must give.

There is no easy path to patience. But two disciplines will help us develop it. The first involves our view of God. If we believe in a sovereign God, then we will become ever more confident that he who began a good work in our brothers and sisters will bring it to completion at the day of Christ (Philippians 1:6). It's possible, of course, to have too much confidence in people, because even the best among us fail. But it's never possible to have too much confidence in God. He has the power and the desire to see that our fellow Christians become like Jesus Christ. We don't have to resign ourselves to their imperfections and weaknesses; neither do we have to take on the responsibility of changing them. Our confidence in God will lead us to pray for them and await the outcome of God's plan to make his strength perfect in their weakness.

The second discipline has to do with how we see ourselves. Patience comes to us more easily when we remind ourselves of what we used to be, and perhaps still are. Impatient people have an inflated view of themselves and probably have a bad memory too. They have forgotten all the foolish decisions they made, the stupid things they said, the petty concerns that occupied their minds. Every so often we need to remind ourselves of what we once were. Many people have been forbearing toward us—our parents, children, teachers, friends, associates. Is it any surprise that God commands us to do the same for others?

I have friends who still shudder when they reminisce about their years in junior high, when their behavior gave a whole new meaning to the word *obnoxious*. I know men who remember what they were like as young husbands when they were as irresponsible as they were passionate. I have met pastors who cringe when they relive their early years in ministry. We will find it less difficult to be patient with people when we remind ourselves of what we were in the distant past.

Consider a young woman who has been raised in a rigid fundamentalist home. She goes to college and discovers that the Christian world is larger than her fundamentalist background. She begins to explore new ideas. Her father is horrified and warns her of the evils of "liberalism." She tries to assure him that she has not deserted the faith, but he considers anything outside fundamentalist beliefs as heresy. His reaction alienates her. She in turn begins to react against his criticism. Soon every discussion turns into an argument. He tries to strong-arm her into submission; she rebels against his authoritarianism. Eventually they can't even talk to each other. The conflict makes him all the more suspicious of liberal ideas and convinces her that all fundamentalists are rigid and narrow.

Forbearance requires that we understand the trajectory of a person's spiritual journey, including our own. All of us have shadows from our past that stalk us, experiences that have shaped how we live today, memories that remind us of what we despise.

Patience enables us to give people time to outgrow and overcome their immaturity. Sometimes people change only through a direct confrontation, when pain and conflict are the inevitable result of love. But in most cases people change naturally through the passing of time. Those who forbear keep an eye on what will someday be.

When I was a young pastor in southern California I attracted several products of the Jesus movement into my youth group. One person in particular seemed to relish the freedom of the counterculture. He wore cutoffs and sandals everywhere, even to morning worship, where he would sometimes sit next to old-timers who dressed in more churchy clothes. He was emotive and expressive in worship. Some church members were irritated by him, but most kept their peace, welcomed him into the church, and gave him room to be himself and to adjust to this new environment. After a couple of years he fell in love with a young woman in the church. Eventually he married her and entered the work force as a professional. Not surprisingly, his dress and behavior began to change, reflecting the more conservative tastes of the business community and the congregation. He adapted to the old-timers, but they also learned from him. The church allowed him to mature, and he contributed significantly to its gradual transformation. Everyone came out the better for it, all because of forbearance.

Not every example, however, leads to such a happy ending. What if people will not change? The passage of time can change people, but it can also harden them, making it almost impossible, outside of a special manifestation of God's power, for them to be transformed. In such cases we must exercise wise judgment. Not everything is worthy of confrontation. Some people—infirm, troubled, depressed, embittered—are best loved as they are unless their problems pose a threat to themselves, others or the cause of Christ. A woman of seventy has spent a lifetime in an unhappy marriage and is now resentful and irritable. A man of forty-five has struggled for a lifetime with severe depression. The prospect of dramatic change in either case is meager. In these and other situations it seems wisest and safest to forbear in hope, reminding ourselves of the wonderful transformation that awaits all Christians in heaven. Sometimes what cannot be done on earth will be done in heaven.

ROOM TO CONTRIBUTE

Jesus does not require perfection before he calls us into service. The Bible shows that fallible people like Abraham, Moses, Esther and David were useful to God. Imperfect Christians can still contribute to the work of Christ. Forbearance is the quality that enables us to affirm and accept their service.

Paul was often troubled by people who resented his success and wanted to undermine his ministry. They proved to be especially aggressive when Paul was not present to defend himself, which occurred often because he spent so much time in jail. Yet he was not helpless. He could counter their influence by writing letters to the churches. One such letter he wrote to the Philippians, who were contending at the time with false apostles. These spiritual pretenders were taking advantage of Paul's absence and advancing their own selfish interests. They had to preach Paul's message, however, in order to win Paul's followers. Thus they proclaimed the same gospel that Paul did, though with motives that were antithetical to the gospel. How did Paul react to the crisis?

> Some proclaim Christ from envy and rivalry, but others from goodwill. These proclaim Christ out of love, knowing that I have been put here for the defense of the gospel; the others proclaim Christ out of selfish ambition, not sincerely but intending to increase my suffering in my imprisonment. What does it matter? Just this, that Christ is proclaimed in every way, whether out of false motives or true; and in that I rejoice. (Philippians 1:15-18)

Paul commended yet a third quality of character to help Christians become forbearing. He charged believers to be lowly in addition to being meek and patient. We, too, must be lowly if we're going to accept service rendered by imperfect people. Lowliness makes us teachable. It helps us realize that we can learn from anyone, even flawed members of the church. Lowly people appreciate others for the unique gifts they bring.

The Greek word that we translate "to forbear" has a secondary meaning: "to listen." The act of listening is indispensable if we want to have true discourse in the church. We learn little, perhaps nothing at all, from people with whom we agree. They may help clarify our thinking and buttress our opinions, but they rarely stretch us to see God's truth in a new light. If we want to learn and grow, we must be willing to listen to those with whom we disagree.

This willingness to listen is especially important when we encounter people who don't share our point of view but who nevertheless call themselves Christian. Failure to forbear at this point leads to impoverishment of mind and spirit. I'm not suggesting that we embrace alien points of view uncritically; that's as dangerous as not listening at all. But I am urging that we listen to, learn from and struggle with Christians whose points of view depart sharply from our own. Some issues may be clear-cut and not require prolonged investigation. But many are not so transparent. They demand careful analysis from many angles. Such exploration may save us from becoming prisoners to our own unexposed prejudices and uncritical ideologies.

While a chaplain at a Christian liberal arts college, I served on a committee that designed a yearly program of reflection on critical issues. We decided one year to explore the theme of Christianity and politics. We wanted to introduce students to a wide range of Christian political thinking, from far left to far right. We heard few comments from our constituency after a speaker from the far right visited the campus. Such was not the case, however, after a speaker from the left addressed us. One supporter of the college threatened to withhold his yearly financial contribution, which amounted to tens of thousands of dollars, if the president did not apologize for this violation of the college's—in actuality, the donor's—political convictions.

The president did not acquiesce. In his reply he explained that though he did not agree with the speaker's point of view, he did believe that it was important for students to be exposed to such thinking because it represented an important and influential voice in the church. The president also invited the donor to attend future forums at which similar issues would be discussed.

Teachableness is also essential when God calls prophets to give a harsh message to the church. We welcome the message of prophets if we agree with them. But are they truly prophets? Several years ago I read an editorial about a commencement speaker at Harvard who was called "prophetic" by one liberal commentator because he denounced fundamentalists. I had to chuckle. What's prophetic about exposing fundamentalists at Harvard? The speaker would have been prophetic if he had denounced the liberal elitism of higher education. Prophets are prophets when they make us uncomfortable.

If we recoil from a prophet's announcement, we tend to use his or her personal weaknesses as an excuse to dismiss the message. For example, it's become common knowledge that Martin Luther King Jr. had a proclivity for infidelity. Still, King's infidelity does not mitigate the power of his convictions and his criticism of the church. His message of justice, equality and freedom is still valid, regardless of his sins. We should not require perfection from prophets before we are willing to listen to their words.

I have observed that disagreement and rivalry tempt us to reduce our opponents to nothing more than the opinions they hold. We must remember that people are complex, multidimensional. There is more to them than their position on, say, abortion. If we allow them to be real people, we might even be surprised by how much their convictions and interests overlap with our own. Like siblings, church people usually fight the meanest against those with whom they have the most in common. We exercise good judgment when we remember what we share in common with our opponents even as we engage them in debate.

Still, some issues are foundational, like the authority of the Bible, the divinity of Christ, the historical nature of the resurrection and the saving nature of Christ's work on the cross. In other words, forbearance has its limits. We must give people room to be, become and contribute—but not limitless room. There is more at stake than the need for space. Truth is also at stake, and so is the health of the church. Somewhere along the line we must draw lines—theological and moral lines.

Jesus himself did not always forbear, and neither did the apostle Paul. Jesus was brutal in his condemnation of the self-righteousness of the Pharisees, and he demanded that sinners repent and "sin no more." Likewise, Paul announced that God would forgive sinners, regardless of how terrible their sin, but he also insisted that they repent. No sin is so bad that God will not forgive it, but no sin is so trivial and innocent that believers do not have to change. As Paul said,

> Do you not know that wrongdoers will not inherit the kingdom of God? Do not be deceived! Fornicators, idolaters, adulterers, male prostitutes, sodomites, thieves, the greedy, drunkards, revilers, robbers—none of these will inherit the kingdom of God. And this is what some of you used to be. (1 Corinthians 6:9-11)

Paul thus commanded the believers in Corinth to pronounce judgment on such evil behavior and to drive out wicked Christians from among them if they were unwilling to repent. Paul put limits on forbearance.

Still, those limits leave lots of room, which is exactly what we should give our brothers and sisters in Christ. Forbearance is where we must start in our relationships with fellow Christians. But as we shall see, it's not where we should end. There is more, much more, that's required if we are to become the loving people that God wants us to be.

5

Forgive One Another

As God's chosen ones, holy and beloved,

clothe yourselves with compassion, kindness,

humility, meekness, and patience. Bear with one

another and, if anyone has a complain against another,

forgive each other; just as the Lord has forgiven you,

so you also must forgive.

COLOSSIANS 3:12-13

A few years ago, I talked with a friend who had just become the pastor of a big city church. His predecessor had left the church in a horrible mess. While serving as the pastor, he had had an affair with the secretary, then divorced his wife in order to marry his lover. He refused to resign from the church and so forced members to choose sides, to ignore the problem or to leave, which many did.

Just a few months ago I read about a controversy in a large church in Spokane that resulted in a major split. Friendships were ruined, families divided, the church's witness damaged. I know of another church that suffered spasms of betrayal because an elder who made his living by managing people's money squandered the savings of dozens of church members in foolish schemes that promised to make him rich. I heard about still another church that publicly humiliated a young couple who were forced to get married due to an unplanned pregnancy. The church's censure alienated family and friends of the couple.

Every one of these situations calls for forgiveness. Every one of these situations makes it very hard to forgive. We've all heard stories of Nazi Germany and cases of brutal murder in which the victims were heroically able to forgive unspeakable evil. Such stories inspire

> *Forgiveness is a manifestation of mercy, given when it's undeserved. Sometimes we must forgive when there is no sign of repentance.*

us, but they don't necessarily speak to circumstances we face day to day. The biblical command to forgive is also addressed to ordinary believers who must learn to love—and therefore forgive—not-so-lovable and not-so-forgivable people who slander, lie, embezzle, commit adultery and betray.

I chose to write about forgiveness before confession because we are called to forgive even when no confession has been made. Forgiveness is a manifestation of mercy, given when it's undeserved. Ideally it's offered to people who are truly sorry for their sin so the broken relationship can be mended. But sometimes we must forgive when there is no sign of repentance. As Jesus said on the cross, "Father, forgive them, for they know not what they are doing."

THE DIFFICULTY

True forgiveness comes hard, especially in the church. I think that's true for two reasons. First, we expect more from Christians. After all, they are disciples of Jesus. Christians disappoint us when they fall short of the standards they are supposed to uphold. Our expectations make failure more inexcusable and unforgivable.

Second, Christians often find it more difficult to admit they are wrong. That, too, makes it harder to forgive them, for there is nothing worse than having to forgive someone unwilling to admit guilt. Christians can be stubbornly self-righteous when they believe they possess God's truth. Their religious self-assurance makes them unreachable, no matter how convincing the evidence against them.

I have a friend who still feels irritation when he remembers his years in ministry on a university campus. He clashed repeatedly with the leaders of another Christian organization. They considered their organization the pivotal ministry—probably the only legitimate ministry—at the university. They refused to consider that their aloofness from other ministries damaged the unity of the church and that their hard-sell techniques trampled people in the name of the gospel. Yet they would not admit to wrong; they would not even consider it. They were too sure they were right. My friend had to forgive them for sin they would not confess.

Offenses that call for forgiveness inflict deep wounds, tempt the offended party to become bitter, create emotional distress and lead to an obsession with the hurt that another caused. They involve complex situations that take time to unravel and resolve. I have talked to many Christians who speak about such experiences from years past as if they'd happened yesterday. The pain lingers. It preoccupies the mind, creates anger and outrage, leads to exhaustion and confusion. It has the power to ruin the spiritual life of the strongest believer. It also has the power to deepen spiritual life like few other experiences can. It all depends, of course, on whether or not we allow God's grace to make us forgiving.

THE OCCASION

The apostle Paul makes it clear that forgiveness must be reserved for offenses that are truly worthy of forgiveness. "As God's chosen ones, holy and beloved, clothe yourselves with compassion, kindness, humility, meekness, and patience. Bear with one another and, if anyone has a complaint against another, forgive each other; just as the Lord has forgiven you, so you also must forgive" (Colossians 3:12-13). It's clear in the passage that not all offenses require forgiveness. That's why Paul exhorts believers to forbear one another first. Irritating idiosyncrasies of personality, immature blunders, foolish but well-intentioned decisions, inexperience—these do not call for forgiveness; they require forbearance instead. People need lots of slack in their journey toward Christian maturity. However unpleasant their behavior can be, they are not really sinning much of the time. Not every bad thing calls for forgiveness.

In the passage above, Paul used the word *complaint* to describe the kinds of offenses that make forgiveness necessary. The Greek word could be translated "reproach" or "worthy of blame." The offense, in other words, has to be bad enough to merit forgiveness.

What constitutes "bad enough" is hard to discern, though, especially in the church. Many people are so sensitive that they take offense at almost anything. They feel rejected when a friend is simply distracted or preoccupied. They feel angry when they are passed over for praise. They feel hurt when someone fails to acknowledge their presence. They think that every private conversation is about them.

I have a pastor friend who learned one day that a member of his church had felt bitter toward him for two years because he had not greeted her properly at a social gathering. He did not sin against her. If there was any sin involved, it was her own self-centeredness. We must beware of diluting the meaning of forgiveness. What we label as sin might in fact be better explained as our own excessive sensitivity.

Forgiveness is required when almost anyone put in the same situation would be as hurt as the offended party was. The offense must violate a universal sense of justice. If a lawyer were hired, she would be able to make a good case before a jury and probably win the case. Sadly, such offenses in the church happen frequently. Power is abused, words are used to wound, confidence is betrayed, churches are divided and relationships destroyed, marriages are broken, money is mismanaged. If the church were a court of law, it would have a full docket of cases to be tried.

Fred and Esther's story is typical. Though active in a local church, they had been struggling with marital problems for years. "Both of us were disappointed with our relationship," Fred told me. "We kept a mental checklist of the faults of the other person, and whenever that person failed to measure up to what we thought a spouse should be, we would add to our checklist. Each of us had a strong case against the other."

Dishonesty in particular poisoned their relationship. "We did not tell each other the whole truth," Esther said.

Fred felt so much pressure to be perfect and to protect his spotless reputation that he refused to tell his wife or anyone else about his disappointments, doubts, fears and temptations. No one knew, for example, that on business trips he would sometimes pick up a *Playboy* magazine and fantasize about having sex with another woman. Esther tended to be more honest, but she communicated her feelings in hurtful ways, using them to get back at Fred for her disappointment in marriage. Consequently, she was not vulnerable to Fred. She, too, had hidden parts of herself.

Fred began to look elsewhere for the love and intimacy he didn't find at home. He started to spend time with a secretary at work who was also having marital difficulties. Eventually they developed a "soul tie," as Fred called it. Later on that led to the physical act of adultery. Though Fred stopped the affair months before Esther found out, he did not break off the relationship with the other woman. Esther never imagined that Fred would be capable of adultery. Still, she was jealous and suspicious.

A friend advised Esther to pray intensively for Fred. Within forty-eight hours after Esther prayed, Fred began to tell the truth and to confess his sin, a process that lasted for several months.

It took Esther far longer to forgive. Her initial impulse was not to forgive but to blame, strike back, condemn. She kept asking him, "How could you do this to me and to the children? How could you do this to God?" She felt betrayed and abused. She was enraged. She wanted justice.

As they eventually discovered, certain factors in their marriage made Fred vulnerable to an affair. Still, as he said to me repeatedly, "There are no good excuses for sin. I was guilty. Esther had justice on her side." Fred could not demand forgiveness because he realized that he didn't deserve it. Esther believed she didn't have to give it. At least at first.

Esther had to learn what many people, including Christians, refuse to acknowledge: that the power to forgive comes from the experience of being a sinner who needs to be forgiven. Jesus taught that forgiving others is in fact impossible if we do not realize how much God has forgiven us. The woman in Luke 7:36-50 loved Jesus much because she knew how much she had been forgiven. As Jesus said, she was forgiven the greater debt, and so showed greater love than did the Pharisee. "The one to whom little is forgiven, loves little," Jesus concluded.

THE COST

Either way you cut it, there is a cost involved. Both forgiveness and unforgiveness exact a price. It's important for us to calculate the cost.

Bill, a seasoned pastor, discovered that cost in the events that led him to resign as the pastor of the church he was serving. He had arrived only a short time before, enthused to begin ministry in a church known for its diversity. On the surface all seemed well. "But what they didn't seem to be conscious of," Bill wrote in a letter to me,

> was the negative spirit of bitterness, of unforgiving avoidance, of petulant criticism which came to characterize the body. When someone is sick long enough, and when the symptoms are easily covered over with fine dress and mascara, or with robust hymn-singing and hearty post-service handshaking, then the sick person doesn't know any longer what it is like to be well. Cantankerous grumbling, spiritual discontent and civil avoidance come to seem "normal."

The members of the pastoral search committee had not told Bill about the church's problems when they called him to be their pastor. "I didn't know it was a troubled church," he wrote.

> The church itself didn't really know. The search committee didn't know at the time of the interviews. At first when grumblings began to surface, I felt deceived. How could these people have called me to minister in a religious community which they pictured as being pro-

gressive and together, when in fact it was fractured by party strife and polarized by ideologies?

For a while Bill lived in the belief that the problem was the church's, not his. The process of restoration began when he was willing to admit his own failure. "After my many years of experiencing church growth in various congregations, the loss of fifteen families left me with a shattered ego and a crisis of self-confidence." Bill was angry because he felt the church had betrayed him and undermined his success.

> There is no room for personal pride, ego-defensiveness, and undue self-confidence in the pastoral role. I needed to learn that. I needed to be taken down a peg to see that without the Spirit of Jesus controlling my life, I was just as much in a carnal fix as that church. The solution for me was death—death to my prideful spirit and confidence in self.

It was this death that enabled him to forgive.

Forgiveness is costly because it requires us to give up the right to get even. The command to forgive runs smack up against our desire to extract payment and to punish the offender. It forces us to let God be God so that his mercy and justice, blended perfectly together, prevail in such a way that not only disciplines but also restores. God is neither brutal nor indulgent. Only he knows how to punish sin without destroying the sinner.

Forgiveness chooses love and mercy over revenge, and it yields to God the right to punish. The apostle Paul explained:

> Do not repay anyone evil for evil, but take thought for what is noble in the sight of all. If it is possible, so far as it depends on you, live peaceably with all. Beloved, never avenge yourselves, but leave room for the wrath of God; for it is written, "Vengeance is mine, I will repay, says the Lord." No, "if your enemies are hungry, feed them; if they are thirsty, give them something to drink; for by doing this you will heap burning coals on their heads." Do not be overcome by evil, but overcome evil with good. (Romans 12:17-21)

The author of Hebrews tells us that God disciplines those whom he loves. Unlike earthly parents, who are often selfish and capricious, God deals with wayward people both harshly and gently. He is committed to helping guilty people repent, be reconciled to former friends and be restored to full relationship with himself. He responds to us out of charity, not brutality.

Still, it's risky to "leave room for the wrath of God," because God might not deal with people as we want and expect. He might not make them suffer as much as we think they deserve. He might not make them suffer at all. He might instead choose to bless them. Thus a former spouse's remarriage might turn out happy, a critic win a following, an incompetent leader stay in office.

Certain factors make the cost of forgiveness almost intolerably high. Particularly painful offenses can raise the cost, like a humiliating betrayal of confidence, mismanagement of church funds that forces cutbacks in ministry, slanderous attacks on character emerging from a power struggle in the church. Some situations—an offender is unaware of wrongdoing or offenses receive public exposure—increase the complexity of the situation and add shame to the pain.

Fred's affair, for example, eventually went public. He resigned from his job and withdrew from the public eye. Esther admitted to me with tears that for several months she did not want to leave the house because she felt so much shame. That made forgiveness all the more costly. Fred had not only hurt her personally; he had also ruined their reputation, damaged many of their friendships and undermined their financial security. The repercussions of his unfaithfulness seemed to go on and on. Esther wondered if they would ever be able to recover and lead a normal life again. She wanted to run away.

Paying the high cost of forgiveness demands strong faith. Faith enables us to believe that God is still God, able to bring good out of evil, however painful the evil has been. Joseph's brothers sold him as a slave to merchants on a caravan to Egypt. Joseph suffered for years from their jealous betrayal. Yet in the end he could say, "You meant it for evil, but God meant it for good." God is a master storyteller; he is able to weave a plot for our lives that uses evil for a greater purpose. God is able to make all things right, however wrong they seem to be. His grace leads to a life of "no regrets" (2 Corinthians 7:5-12). He is so great that he can turn ashes into bread, a desert into a fertile field, suffering into triumph. It takes time for him to do this great work, of course. Only faith will sustain us as we wait for God to heal and to restore.

However costly forgiveness is, it does not compare with the cost of un-forgiveness. In the midst of her unforgiveness, Esther began to observe peo-

> **However costly forgiveness is, it does not compare with the cost of unforgiveness.**

ple she knew who were holding a grudge, harboring resentment, plotting revenge. She noticed the misery of their lives, their twisted perspective, their sickness of body and soul. She learned that they were slaves to the past, prisoners of their wretched memories, obsessed with getting even. They were angry, anxious, joyless, overly sensitive. Unforgiveness was killing them. They could take comfort in being right. They could justify wanting to strike back. But was being right worth it? Did unforgiveness bring that much pleasure? Was their world better because it was empty of mercy?

Unforgiveness condemns us to live forever in the dungeon of the past. The memory serves only to remind us of what went wrong, of the hurt we received. We caress that painful memory. We find a strange happiness in thinking about it. It finally poisons us. The apostle Paul described what happens to the person who has given in to unforgiveness. "And do not grieve the Holy Spirit of God, with which you were marked with a seal for the day of redemption. Put away from you all bitterness and wrath and anger and wrangling and slander, together with all malice" (Ephesians 4:30-31).

Unforgiveness leads to wrath, which makes us quick to accuse and ready to explode the moment we're crossed; wrath makes us quick to punish; wrangling engenders quarrelsomeness; slander is the crude attempt to turn other people against the offender; malice makes us wish evil on another person. Unforgiveness may get its way. It may cause hurt, inflict punishment, heap blame. Yet its greatest victim is the unforgiving self. Maybe that's why

Jesus was so severe with people who refused to forgive. He understood how destructive it was for everyone, especially the unforgiving person.

THE LIMITATIONS

Forgiveness can't do everything. It has power, but its power is limited. It pushes us in the direction of restored relationships, but by itself it will not get us all the way there. More is needed, much more.

For example, forgiveness does not release offenders from the need to take personal responsibility for the sin committed. Forgiveness assumes that people are responsible for their sinful actions and holds them accountable for what they have done. Forgiveness bestows the honor on people of taking their wrongdoing seriously. We must forgive them because they know better.

Forgiveness does not absolve offenders from guilt. Only God has the power to absolve; only he can decide the fate of every person's soul. Human forgiveness does not bestow divine forgiveness. A new Christian may have to forgive a father for abuse; that does not guarantee that the father's soul is now secure. A Christian leader may have to forgive a board of elders for stubborn opposition; that does not mean that all things have been made right between the board and God.

We forgive in a relative sense; we have the power to restore the broken relationship between ourselves and the offender. God forgives in an ultimate sense; he has the power to restore the broken relationship with himself. The Pharisees were furious with Jesus because he assumed a prerogative that belongs only to God. He forgave people for sins they had committed against other people (Mark 2:1-12). That's something only God can do, which of course is why Jesus could—and did—forgive.

Forgiveness does not deliver the offender from the consequences of sinful actions. I remember saying often to my mother while I was growing up, "But I thought you forgave me! Why am I still being punished?" That's a little boy's crude theology. Sometimes adults don't do much better. Students who are disciplined at our college for some violation often say, with wearisome predictability, "I thought that this was a Christian college. You believe in forgiveness, don't you? Then why am I still being suspended?" For some reason people believe that forgiveness miraculously erases the consequences of the past, breaking the connection between past wrong and present circumstances, as if the law of sowing and reaping no longer applied.

But it does. Jesus' death on the cross was a real death because sin has real consequences, no matter how repentant we are. Jesus died to pay the penalty for sin. He took on himself the consequences we deserved. The cross brings justice and mercy together in one event. Someone had to die; that's justice. Someone died in place of the guilty party; that's mercy.

Forgiveness cannot erase the past. Esther knew that if she did forgive Fred, that would not get his job back. Nor would her forgiveness restore Fred's spotless reputation. The shame and humiliation would not disappear overnight. Some decisions have permanent consequences—immoral behavior leading to loss of church office, church conflict engendering a major church split, unwise financial decisions crippling the church with severe indebtedness. Forgiveness is a wonderful gift. Still, it cannot save us from having to face the consequences of our sinful behavior, which can pursue us with unrelenting ferocity.

THE POSSIBILITIES

Yet forgiveness can accomplish great good in the church if we understand its true meaning. Forgiveness means releasing offenders from the consequences of their behavior *as it affects us*. It cancels the debt they owe us and saves them from having to pay us back. It absorbs the wrongdoing. Forgiveness reestablishes the relationship, at least from our end. It restores communication and, under the right circumstances, can restore friendship. It uses the past as a means of strengthening the relationship, not destroying it. Forgiveness is like the growth of a tree that envelops a wound in the trunk, so that what once threatened the tree's life becomes its place of greatest strength. Forgiveness ultimately means that we wish offenders well and hope that our relationship with them will grow. We want them to prosper. We pray God's grace and peace on them. We choose to love them, even though they do not deserve it.

Forgiveness enables a woman who desires to hold the office of pastor to understand her opponents' fears, forgive them for their opposition and reach out to them in love, whether or not they are willing to change their minds. Similarly, it enables a pastor of a mainline church who is criticized by angry feminists in the congregation to view their circumstances with compassion, overlook their bitterness and hostility, and serve them as best he can, whether or not they are open to his pastoral leadership. Forgiveness empowers us to transcend the situation so that we listen, learn, love and serve even when offenders show no signs of remorse and change.

Forgiveness also takes time. There are no shortcuts. We begin the process by admitting our hurt. We must feel the pain and voice the outrage. It helps no one to whitewash the problem. Forgiveness is not the same as excusing the offense, suppressing conflict, accepting the offender or tolerating the behavior. These may have a place, but they are not forgiveness.

We must come to the point of stating that there is no reason the offense had to happen, there is every reason it should not have happened, and there is good reason for us to feel hurt and angry. So before a woman can forgive church members who oppose her calling to church office, she must first recognize and feel the full effects of the wrong done her. Likewise, before a male pastor can forgive angry feminists for attacking him simply because he is male, he must first experience the injustice of the unfair attack.

That's where the journey of forgiveness must begin. But it's not where it should end. The goal is genuine forgiveness, which always surfaces in love.

Forgiveness in the end is an act of mercy and grace. Eventually Esther wanted to see her relationship with Fred healed. She chose the way of forgiveness over the way of revenge. She gave up the right to punish Fred, extract a payment, relive the ugly details and reopen the wounds. She decided that harmony and wholeness were better than anguish and hatred. She started to invest again in the relationship. She wanted to make it stronger than it had been before. Though she attached no conditions to her forgiveness, she did challenge Fred to search his own soul to discover what had made him vulnerable and how he could protect himself next time around.

I was deeply impressed by Fred and Esther's story. If they had the option, they would return to the past and live it over differently. Obviously they can't. So they have done the next best thing. They have invited God into the past so that it can be made right. Their story has moved many people. It has helped to make peace in other Christians' marriages that were broken by infidelity or hostility. It has inspired husbands and wives to settle old scores, to live transparently, to deal with present and past problems. Their story is leading to a happy ending because Esther chose forgiveness over bitterness and revenge.

Bill chose forgiveness too. His situation was more complex because it involved so many people, some of whom were unwilling to admit any responsibility for causing disunity in the church. Bill had to forgive people who did not believe that they were guilty—most of the congregation, in fact. Yet his forgiveness set in motion a series of events that brought healing to the entire body. Forgiveness, as we shall see in the next chapter, led to confession. And confession reconciled relationships. Such is the power of forgiveness. It unleashes the grace of God.

6

Confess Sin to and
Pray for One Another

Are any among you suffering? They should pray. Are any cheerful?

They should sing songs of praise. Are any among you sick?

They should call for the elders of the church and have them pray

over them, anointing them with oil in the name of the Lord.

The prayer of faith will save the sick, and the Lord will raise them up;

and anyone who has committed sins will be forgiven.

Therefore confess your sins to one another, and pray for one another,

so that you may be healed. The prayer of the righteous is powerful and effective.

JAMES 5:13-16

I once witnessed the power of confession in a church embroiled in controversy. A leader of the church had been putting tremendous pressure on lay-
people to do the work of ministry. His philosophy troubled a number of
church members who had different ideas of what clergy and laity ought to
do. Their disagreement was aggravated by the leader's strong and demanding personality. His critics accused him of extracting outrageous commitments of time, energy and loyalty from his followers. They also said that he

acted like a messiah, thinking that how people responded to him reflected how they responded to Jesus Christ. The accusations and acrimony were forcing the two parties toward a showdown.

One evening during prayer at a worship service, the leader took the microphone, as was the procedure for anyone who wanted to request prayer, and told the congregation of his personal struggle against the sin of pride, of the enormous ego that had created such anguish in his life and of the drive for control that made people dislike him. He admitted his loneliness and pain, and he expressed his longing to be gentle and humble. Then he asked the congregation to forgive him and pray for him. His act of confession exposed his own need to the church and invited the church to see him as a sinner in need of grace. And it gave his opponents the freedom to admit that they were at fault too.

Confession levels the playing field of the church. It mitigates conflicts that threaten to destroy us and disarms our opponents by demonstrating the way of humility to them. It reduces us to the needy people we are, regardless of where we come down on the issues. It reminds us—everyone, really—that weakness in the presence of God has dignity and integrity that human strength cannot comprehend.

A FUTILE QUEST

Throughout the history of the church, Christian theologians and pastors have observed a deep need in the human heart that only God can fill. Human nature has an incompleteness, a sense of alienation and estrangement that goes to the depth of our being, a sense that something is profoundly wrong inside us. It's the human condition. We were made to become like God, but we were also made to depend totally on God. No one can take God's place in our lives. No one can do for us what God alone can. If we do not learn this lesson in the course of our life, we will spend a lifetime trying to find a replacement for God—which is as foolish as trying to run our bodies on something besides oxygen, water and food.

The whole world is groaning because human beings have tried to put something in God's place. We see the effects everywhere: strained marriages, rebellious children, perverse imagination, smallness of spirit, injustice and violence in society, sickness of body and mind, addictions of every kind. The leaders of the Reformation used the phrase "total depravity" to describe the extent to which sin reaches; it touches every area of life. We might not be as bad as we could be, but every part of us has some degree of badness in it. We may know the problem is there, but we can't seem to solve it. There is no unstained area of our lives to which we can appeal. We are fallen creatures.

The self-help movement has raised the expectation in many people that they have the power within themselves to overcome the dark side of human nature, to take control of their lives and to reach perfection. It has only reinforced our obsession with power and control. Self-help implies that if people learn the right philosophy and practice the right techniques, they will be able to manage time, money, diet, thoughts, feelings, people, circumstances and problems, until they reach the point of complete mastery.

We can gain much from the self-help movement. Who doesn't stand in need of conquering bad habits and overcoming nagging problems? I for one have benefited greatly from books and seminars that have taught me how to manage my time, how to budget my limited financial resources, how to work with problem people, how to turn negative circumstances into positive opportunities for personal growth. Self-help empowers people to live more creatively, responsibly and happily.

But there is a problem in human nature that self-help can't touch—the problem of sin. Sin runs deeper than the surface problems that techniques can help us to overcome. If anything, self-help can actually exacerbate sin by deluding us into thinking that we have the power to solve it. It's possible to become a child of hell even as we strive to become a child of heaven. If self-help makes us think that God is unnecessary, then it's worse than the prob-

> *There is a problem in human nature that the self-help movement can't touch— the problem of sin.*

lems that it helps us to conquer. Jesus offered a different way of exposing and eradicating sin: confession and prayer.

THE FELLOWSHIP OF SINNERS

The mutuality command of confession and prayer addresses the debilitating effects of sin in human life, whether it be our own sin or someone else's. Confession exposes us for the sinners we are and opens us to God's grace. Confession makes the church a community for sinners instead of pious saints. It gives us the freedom to be vulnerable and honest rather than pretentious and hypocritical. Prayer, in turn, enables us to receive God's healing power so we can become whole and healthy, not because we have mastered self-help techniques but because we have learned to seek God, trust his goodness and embrace his gracious provision.

In *Life Together* Dietrich Bonhoeffer argued that mutual confession constitutes the "break-through" to fellowship. Confession brings sin to light, where it's exposed and then covered by the grace of God. Where sin goes unacknowledged, grace remains untapped, an abstract idea that does not touch and transform our experience. According to Bonhoeffer, we must confess our sin in the presence of a brother or sister in Christ. Confession makes us sinners before one another, breaks us of our self-righteousness and enables us to become a fellowship of sinners. Thus we become the church that is founded on Christ's righteousness, not our own.

Of all the mutuality commands, confession and prayer pose the greatest risk to ourselves and perhaps the greatest hope for the church to become a loving community. Controversy and conflict engender a defensive and accusatory spirit in the church. We criticize our opponents' weaknesses and applaud our own strengths; they do likewise. We forget what sinners we are, however right our particular perspective might be. We forget that being right is not the only goal of Christians—especially not at the expense of Christian virtue.

Confession forces us to own up to our sin and not to use others' wrongness to excuse our own. Confession reminds us that we desperately need the grace of God. It makes us weak and vulnerable, exposing our underbellies to the church and revealing that we are not so high and mighty after all. This is risky because it yields ground to our opponents. It gives them the edge.

Still, it's a risk worth taking. Confession may put us at the mercy of our opponents, but it also puts us under the mercy of God. In my mind it's better to lose power and gain our own soul than to have power at the price of our soul. Confession gains the soul, for it leads us to the cross, where we can find forgiveness and hope.

JOURNEY TO WHOLENESS

The mutuality command of confession and prayer is found in the book of James, at the end of a series of injunctions James gives to his readers:

> Are any among you suffering? They should pray. Are any cheerful? They should sing songs of praise. Are any among you sick? They should call for the elders of the church and have them pray over them, anointing them with oil in the name of the Lord. The prayer of faith will save the sick, and the Lord will raise them up; and anyone who has committed sins will be forgiven. Therefore confess your sins to one another, and pray for one another, so that you may be healed. (James 5:13-16)

The passage assumes a connection between spiritual health and physical health. Sin causes sickness; confession and prayer lead to healing. The kind of relationship we have with God determines the quality of our life in the world. Sin has consequences, just as forgiveness does. Those consequences are physical as well as spiritual.

The Bible links sin with sickness in other passages as well. The lame man in Mark 2 had to be forgiven before he could be healed. The apostle Paul argued that some believers in the church at Corinth had become ill and had even died because they had sinned by taking Communion in an unworthy manner (1 Corinthians 11:27-30). David believed that unconfessed sin erodes the human spirit, causing exhaustion and anguish.

While I kept silence, my body wasted away
> through my groaning all day long.
For day and night your hand was heavy upon me;
> my strength was dried up as by the heat of summer. (Psalm 32:3-4)

As mental health professionals have shown, guilt often undermines good health, leading to such physical maladies as asthma, sleeplessness, nervousness, arthritis, ulcers and headaches. When the spirit is not right with God, the body pays the price.

The link between sin and sickness does not imply, however, that sickness is *always* the consequence of personal sin. Sickness is also the result of the world's sin in general. Jesus did not indicate that all the sick people he met deserved to be sick because they had sinned. In one instance, in fact, he said outright that a man's blindness was *not* the result of his sin or his parents' sin; rather it was for the glory of God (John 9).

James links sin and sickness because sin, whether ours or someone else's, takes its toll on the body, mind and spirit, thus damaging what God has designed for human life. The way to reverse the destructive cycle is through mutual confession and prayer. Confession admits wrongdoing. Prayer asks for restoration and healing. God is the one who acts to make us whole. Thus just as sin leads to sickness, so confession and prayer lead to forgiveness and wholeness.

CONFESSION AND RESTORATION

When we confess to the people whom we have offended and from whom we need forgiveness, we imply that we are responsible for our wrongdoing and want to restore the relationship. As Jesus said, "When you are offering your gift at the altar, if you remember that your brother or sister has something against you, leave your gift there before the altar and go; first be reconciled to your brother or sister, and then come and offer your gift" (Matthew 5:23-24). Confession holds the promise of reconciling broken relationships and healing wounds in the body of Christ. Jesus commands us to confess our faults to those hurt by them, regardless of whether they are also guilty and intend to respond in kind. There are no conditions attached to this command, which makes Jesus' words difficult to obey. It is natural to wait until the other party is willing to admit fault as well. Such unwillingness to act first often keeps Christians from obeying this command at all.

In the last chapter I told the story of a pastor, Bill, who faced the difficult task of forgiving his congregation for divisiveness and criticism. He also realized that he had failed them and needed to take responsibility for the sins he had committed. He decided in his discouragement and brokenness to admit his failures openly and resign from the church. As he wrote:

> So it happened. The day came when I decided to leave the ministry and take a position in teaching. Never did I dream this kind of defeat could happen to me. I was broken and admitted to the elders and congregation my failure and my decision to seek other work.

Strangely, his decision to confess his sins charged him with new energy and boldness.

> Along with my brokenness came a strange new courage, boldness to tell the council and congregation how I saw the whole situation in all its tragedy. Never had I dared be this honest. What would they think? I had nothing to lose anymore. I had already given over this job and my career. Reactions didn't matter anymore. What freedom!

Freedom for him; repentance, as it turned out, for them.

> What an amazing response from the people: one by one dropping to their knees. They were dying, too! One by one getting up out of their pews and going over to someone with whom they sought reconciliation. Forgiveness was happening! In the church! God Almighty, could it be!
>
> The explanation was simple. It was a miracle of healing brought by a fresh outpouring of the Holy Spirit, sparked by brokenness, absolute honesty, confession and forgiveness. On all sides. God led me to stay with this church and ministry.

His confession invited forgiveness, and healing followed. The miracle continued for some time. Relationships were restored, membership loss stopped, undercurrents of discontent and criticism were stilled. Bill's preaching became more honest, simple and direct, the congregation's response more genuine. The church became a community of sinners for the first time. And it all started because someone was willing to risk everything by confessing his sin.

The more general application of this command involves confession of sin before brothers and sisters in Christ who are in a position to impart grace to us, to support us in our weakness and to help us overcome our sinful inclinations. Confession in this case forces us to be honest about ourselves, makes our faith authentic and leads us into the light of the gospel.

But we recoil from this kind of exposure. We fear being known as sinners and tend therefore to hide behind a front of false piety. We project an image of ourselves as strong and pious Christians, though looming behind the image are doubts, addictions, fears and failures.

Christian leaders in particular face enormous pressure to perform as models of perfection before their adoring congregations or organizations. As a consequence they often experience profound loneliness, wanting desperately to be known for the sinners they are but feeling terrified by the prospect of being found out. So they feel pressure to demonstrate that they have conquered all sin and stand before the people of God as examples of faith and obedience. They deny their own raw humanity for the sake of their ministry.

That impulse to be perfect before the world only increases their vulnerability to sin, which they can't admit to anyone else or maybe even to themselves. Until it's too late. Over the past few years the church has witnessed the moral failure of many prominent Christian leaders whose secret sins were finally exposed after months and even years of deception. They might have followed a different path if at least a few of their friends in the church had known of their struggles and helped them face their weaknesses squarely. Their heroism isolated them from the church and forced them to struggle alone. Appearance became more important than truth, image more important than authenticity.

Christian leaders, like other members of the church, need a safe place for themselves where they can admit their problems and receive grace through the ministry of the body of Christ. They, too, are called to be full members of the church, even though they may be leaders of it. They, too, are accountable to others, need their support and love and require the ministry of compassion when they are broken. They, too, must confess their sins and experience forgiveness.

Several years ago a student came to see me saying that he had a secret to tell. When he was in junior high he had a serious acne problem on his back. His classmates used to tease him about it. One day he returned from football practice later than his teammates. When he entered the shower, only a few others remained. They congregated in a corner, whispering. Suddenly they jumped him, wrestled him to the ground and, taking a safety pin, began to prick the acne on his back. They told him that they were going to help him get rid of it. They laughed, making jokes about his back and claiming to be his only true friends. Then they left him lying on the shower floor. He was overcome with rage and shame. He never told anyone about his humiliation until the day he entered my office. He sobbed throughout the story. Then he confessed his deep bitterness toward his assailants. Once the truth was out, the emotion spent, the confession made, he stood up a new man, having received the healing grace of God.

Despite the healing power of confession, it nevertheless needs to have limits. While Christians must confess their sin, they should not be indiscriminate with whom they talk and lurid in how they tell it. Not everything should be said, and not everyone should be told. Confession should get to the point and focus on the real problem, sparing the gory details that awaken curiosity and sidetrack people. If adultery is the sin, then adultery should be confessed. But that doesn't mean the person doing the confessing should take twenty minutes to describe every detail. Nor should that person announce the sin to the world. The circle of those who hear should include only those who have the right or responsibility to hear: spouse, support group, pastor. Not necessarily the whole church. Private sins require a small circle privy to the confession, public sins a large circle.

Confession also needs to have a goal: to restore the sinner to full fellowship with God and the church. That requires us to focus on the root problem so that confession leads not only to forgiveness but also to insight, self-knowledge, discipline and victory. We need to learn the why after we have admitted the where, when, who and how. Confession mandates that we not only repent of a past misdeed but also pursue a future plan of action. Confession "puts off" past sins; restoration engenders a new mind and "puts on" new behavior (Ephesians 4:22-24 RSV). The old way of sin must yield to the new way of godliness. Confession should eventually lead to transformation.

Finally, confession may uncover problems that require the expertise of mental health professionals. Confession assumes personal responsibility for sin. But the root of the problem may involve more than a rebellious will. It may also involve past traumas, genetic challenges, even mental illness. Therapy does not eliminate the need for confession; it supplements confession by probing the reasons for the sin and by exploring new strategies for healing and growth. The church and the mental health community should be allies, not enemies, in the quest for spiritual wholeness.

PRAYER AND HEALING

James tells us to confess sin and pray for one another that we may be healed. Full restoration requires prayer as well as confession. If confession exposes our sin and brokenness, prayer gives us access to the healing power of God.

Prayer is perhaps the greatest service we can render our fellow believers. That may surprise activists who insist that Christians serve broken people best through acts of justice and mercy. They take their responsibilities as followers of Jesus seriously, just as they take the Bible's criticism of apathy seriously. They do not want to fail their needy brothers and sisters, like those who simply dismiss the problem with a casual "God bless you. Go on your

way now. Be warmed and filled. I'll be praying for you" (James 2:15-16).
They recoil from the sin of indifference.

But prayerful people are cautious about overestimating their powers to
meet people's deepest needs. They do not want to be presumptuous. That
does not mean they neglect their God-
given duty to serve, to bear burdens
and the like. But they recognize that
some needs run so deep, some problems become so severe, that God and
only God can provide the solution, for
God alone is sufficient. People need to
know God, to receive his grace, to ex-
perience his healing power. No human ministry is adequate to touch people
at the deepest levels of their being. That's why we must pray. Prayer does not
replace practical ministry; it's the most effective expression of practical ministry. Prayer lifts people into the presence of God.

> *If confession exposes our sin and brokenness, prayer gives us access to the healing power of God.*

My own experience over the past fifteen years affirms the importance of
prayer. I have benefited in many ways from the church's practical help since
my wife, mother and daughter died in an accident. People have served me,
comforted me and encouraged me. But over time I have appreciated the
ministry of prayer the most. It did not take me long to get back on my feet
and learn how to manage my life well. I am as self-sufficient as they come.
Yet I feel more needy now than ever before, largely because I am more aware
now of the human condition—*my* human condition. I struggle with profound questions, nagging doubts, occasional loneliness. I have needs no human being can fill, problems no practical advice will solve. That's why I tell
people to pray for me, and why I pray so often for others. All of us need people to believe for us when we can't muster the faith ourselves, to intervene
before God on our behalf, to pray the grace and love of God into our soul.
Prayer does something for us that literally nothing else can do.

A number of members at our church have been called to the ministry of
prayer. They pray for hours every week and meet together regularly to pray

for each other, for needy members of the congregation and for the church around the world. Sometimes they sit in silence and listen to God until God gives them the prayers to pray. They pray as a community for one need at a time until there is discernment and agreement among them. They keep in regular contact with the people for whom they are praying. They consider prayer their most important ministry in the church.

We must pray for our enemies too, especially for our enemies in the church—not for their defeat but for their salvation. They need the grace of God, as we do; they need God's help, as we do; they need to know God's truth, as we do. Sometimes prayer is the only ministry we can offer our Christian opponents because it's the only ministry they will receive from us. They may reject our welcome, service, encouragement, admonition. They may avoid us altogether. But they cannot spurn our prayers. The effectiveness of prayer does not depend on how well we get along with another person. It depends only on God's grace and power.

Prayer for enemies is a profound act of love. Jesus said:

> You have heard that it was said, "You shall love your neighbor and hate your enemy." But I say to you, Love your enemies and pray for those who persecute you, so that you may be children of your Father in heaven; for he makes his sun rise on the evil and on the good, and sends rain on the righteous and on the unrighteous. (Matthew 5:43-45)

The commitment to pray for enemies reminds us that our opponents, including those in the church, are human beings with problems like our own. Regardless of their position on an issue, they battle sins of flesh and spirit, find it hard sometimes to trust God, fight a losing war against mortality, and wonder occasionally whether their faith is real and God is true. They are more complex than the opinions they hold, more needy than the way they appear in public, more vulnerable to sin and evil than they would ever let on. They are our brothers and sisters in Christ, whether we like them or not, whether we trust them or not. We must be as generous with our prayers as God is with rain and sunshine, which he sends to everyone regardless of worthiness. Conversation in the church may sometimes fail, negotiations break down, affection dissipate in the heat of conflict, mutual respect deteriorate. But we can always pray for our opponents.

Confession exposes; prayer heals. Confession takes responsibility for wrongdoing; prayer asks God to help us do what is right. Confession acknowledges the human condition; prayer draws on the transcendent power of God. Confession admits to sin; prayer leads us to salvation. The two belong together as one mutuality command. Confession challenges us to risk being weak and vulnerable before our brothers and sisters in Christ. We can of course choose not to confess, because in many cases no one will ever know our sins. But in the long run we will suffer loss, for we will not be known and still loved for the sinners we are, nor will we receive the grace of God through the ministry of others. Prayer, in turn, requires us to intercede on behalf of those who have been weak and vulnerable before us. This mutuality command appeals directly to God, who alone has the power to forgive, restore and heal broken sinners—such as we all are.

7

Serve One Another

In its simplest form, service means that one person cares for another person in need. Alice was one such person. She roomed across the hall from Tricia during her freshman year of college. Tricia was a bright, happy, friendly young woman, competent and successful academically, active in her church and busy every day of the week. But Tricia had muscular dystrophy, which left her with only partial use of her arms and no use of her legs. She lived in a wheelchair.

At the end of the year Alice asked Tricia if she could be her roommate. Though surprised, Tricia agreed. Every day Alice dressed Tricia, combed her hair, made her bed, washed her clothes, turned her over during the night, gave her a shower, took her to the bathroom, helped her get exercise and maintained her motorized wheelchair. Such service was demanding, but it became a part of the daily schedule.

"There were days," Alice told me, "when I did not feel like serving. These feelings were usually followed by guilt. Tricia depended on me and could not function without my help. I had to put aside my selfish feelings and meet her needs first. If I did not change my attitude, but rather went through the motions to help her, Tricia would sense that through the way I handled her. I soon learned that serving is not only what you do, it's an attitude of the heart."

Alice came to do more than take care of Tricia's personal needs. She carried Tricia up flights of stairs so she could attend a friend's surprise birthday party. She even took her sledding. "In a push and one big whoosh," Alice said, "we were speeding down the hill. We ended with a wipe-out at the bottom of the hill and snow in our faces. We had never laughed so hard! Going down was quick. Carrying her back up the hill was a task, but well worth it!"

Alice is one of my heroes. She helped make it possible for Tricia to earn a college degree and prepare for a meaningful vocation as an elementary school teacher. Tricia had all the abilities she needed; she had a winsome personality and a happy heart. But she needed someone to meet her basic needs. Alice was that person.

To serve one another in the body of Christ is to commit our resources—time, money, energy and expertise—to meet the practical needs of fellow believers. Two different words are translated as "serve" from the Greek. We could translate one "to be a slave of," the other word "to wait on." Service implies that we wait on other people, as if we are choosing to be their slave. It means we devote ourselves to meet the needs of people overlooked or exploited in our society.

Service is necessary for two groups of people in particular. The first is people who cannot function as productive disciples if they don't receive help. Some Christians are kept from doing the will of God not because they don't want to but because they aren't able to. They lack basic necessities—steady income, transportation, child care, medical attention—that allow them to live productively. Service takes care of these practical needs so that people can do what God wills and they want.

The second group of people who need service comprises those who, without the help of others, would not survive at all. Children in orphanages need service. Old people in nursing homes need service. Severely disabled people need service. When I was an interim pastor in Chicago, I met a woman who took care of her invalid husband for ten years. He was completely incapacitated, unable to move, eat or talk. He was as motionless and expressionless as a block of wood. Yet she fed him every day, massaged him and moved him so he wouldn't get bedsores, invited visitors into his room, played music and talked to him throughout the day. She had little hope that he would recover. But that did not keep this remarkable woman from serving him faithfully and without complaint.

THAT ALL THINGS BE EQUAL

Service means sacrifice. It requires us to give so that as we learn to live with less (time, money, energy, opportunity, advancement), others in need will have more. But it must be *voluntary* sacrifice. In Galatians 5:13-14 Paul enjoins believers to use their freedom in Christ to serve one another. Freedom, then, sets the stage for service. Gratitude for God's gifts will inspire us to use our gifts for others; freedom from compulsion will make us eager to sacrifice for somebody else's sake.

Paul suggested that the goal of such service is equality. In his second letter to the Christian community at Corinth, he encouraged believers there to fulfill the promise they had made at an earlier time to collect money for the poor in Jerusalem. He admired their willingness, but he wanted them to match that willingness with action.

> For if the eagerness is there, the gift is acceptable according to what one has—not according to what one does not have. I do not mean that there should be relief for others and pressure on you, but it is a question of a fair balance between your present abundance and their need, so that their abundance may be for your need, in order that there may be a fair balance. (2 Corinthians 8:12-14)

In Paul's mind, the gospel moves those who have much to invest it in those who have little until all things become equal.

This quest for equality has potential for uniting the church. If we see ourselves as stewards of God's gifts rather than owners, we will be more willing to invest in the church, striving to help those who have less get more—not simply more money, but more knowledge, compassion, wholeness and opportunity. The advantages some Christians have because of natural endowment, background, opportunity and hard work should be used as a resource to lift other Christians up, not put them in their place. People who become sensitive to suffering in the world through their study and travels should not complain about insensitive and compassionless people in their local churches but instead spearhead programs that expose others to the world's needs. Likewise, people who become aware of human brokenness through their own journey toward wholeness should not condemn self-sufficient people in the church but instead help them recognize their responsibility to contribute to healing. The ministry of service promises to unite the church in the greater purpose of creating a healthy body.

IT SHALL NOT BE SO AMONG YOU

The Bible teaches that servanthood is every Christian's duty. But it speaks most forcefully about servanthood when it addresses leaders. When his disciples began to argue about who would be the greatest among them, Jesus said:

> You know that among the Gentiles those whom they recognize as their rulers lord it over them, and their great ones are tyrants over them. But it is not so among you; but whoever wishes to become great among you must be your servant, and whoever wishes to be first among you must be slave of all. For the Son of Man came not to be served but to serve, and to give his life a ransom for many. (Mark 10:42-45)

Jesus himself set an example of servanthood when, the night before his crucifixion, he washed the disciples' feet (John 13) and then commanded them to follow his example. Peter must have gotten the message. He exhorted the elders of the churches "to tend the flock of God that is in your charge, exercising the oversight, not under compulsion but willingly, as God would have you do it—not for sordid gain but eagerly. Do not lord it over those in your charge, but be examples to the flock" (1 Peter 5:2-3).

Jesus envisioned a community of disciples who would dare to move downward instead of upward, to retreat from ambition so others could get ahead. He of course was the quintessential example. Paul wrote, "For you know the generous act [grace] of our Lord Jesus Christ, that though he was rich, yet for your sakes he became poor, so that by his poverty you might become rich" (2 Corinthians 8:9). Though Jesus was in the form of God, Paul declared to the Philippians, he did not count equality with God a thing to be grasped but emptied himself and became a servant, even to the point of sacrificial death (Philippians 2:5-11).

> *Jesus envisioned a community of disciples who would dare to move downward instead of upward.*

If anyone had the right not to sacrifice himself, Jesus did. Yet he offered his life for our sake. We too are to count others as better than ourselves and seek their welfare in Christ.

Like leaders, gifted people in the church—musicians, preachers, writers, scholars, managers—are not exempt from servanthood. Lynda and I were in the final stages of adopting a special needs child when the accident occurred. Adoption would have given us a fifth child, and Lynda had not eliminated the possibility of a sixth, even though she was forty-two at the time. Some people raised questions about this decision, especially as it would have inevitably affected Lynda's schedule and career. She was a gifted leader and musician who could have excelled in her career and gained a high profile in the community.

"Why another baby?" they asked. "Couldn't you use your gifts in a better way?"

Lynda always replied the same way: "I can't think of a better way to use my abilities than in service to my children."

Some people assume—wrongly—that gifted people are excused from serving and sacrificing and are expected instead to develop their abilities as much as possible rather than neglect them for some ostensibly lesser cause. Yet that's what servanthood sometimes requires. A father might sacrifice career advancement to care for his children; a prominent church leader might take a sabbatical to teach Sunday school to first-graders; a talented coach might sacrifice a lucrative job opportunity to start a recreation program in the inner city. Jesus said we would be judged by how we cared for "the least of these," the people we tend to overlook as we climb to the top. Sometimes we find opportunity to use our gifts in service; at other times we have to let them lie dormant for the sake of service.

TIME, MONEY AND EXPERTISE

George Barna argues that time, not money, has become the most important commodity in Western culture. I can testify to the value of time. My children are all grown, but I can well remember how little time I had as a single parent when they were still at home. I managed the home, taught at the college, volunteered at church, coached soccer, sat in on music lessons and took care of endless chores at home. I battled frustration and resented interruptions, of which there were many.

But servanthood takes time. Mowing the lawn of a widow takes time, visiting the sick at a hospital takes time, volunteering at a clinic for low-income families takes time, spring cleaning at church takes time, organizing a Vacation Bible School takes time.

What do we do when we feel like we don't have time to serve? First, we must consider the impact of every decision we make. Purchases, commitments, responsibilities, hobbies and projects all contain hidden costs. We must be ruthlessly realistic about those costs. Every home improvement project I've begun has taken triple the time I anticipated. Leisure activities I enjoy often take far more time than I estimate. I have friends who bought a cabin as a family getaway. As a vacation spot, it's been wonderful. As a piece of property requiring upkeep, it's been a drain on time and resources.

Second, we must simplify our lives as much as possible. Renting a cabin may be more convenient than owning one, providing rest without the responsibility of upkeep. Saying no to all but the essential commitments may release time in our schedules for more service. Careful planning of the calendar may protect us from getting too busy at the wrong times of year—say, during late summer when we need a rest, or around the holidays.

Third, we must make service a habit and build it into our weekly schedules. Service will fit into the rhythm of our lives only if we make it a regular priority, such as when we volunteer to teach Sunday school for an entire year or tend the nursery once a month. If service is not planned, it's the first thing to go when our time is pinched.

Time is not the only important commodity for those who want to serve— so is money. Money is necessary for transportation, supplies, education, child care, salaries, administration. However willing, however committed, however organized we are, we will not succeed in serving without money.

The wealthy have the greatest resources at their disposal but often have the most difficulty giving it up. Who are the wealthy? If we take into account how people in India, Nigeria, Bangladesh and South America live, middle-class Christians in America are wealthy. The Bible warns us to be wary of wealth. Paul exhorted Timothy:

> But those who want to be rich fall into temptation and are trapped by many senseless and harmful desires that plunge people into ruin and destruction. For the love of money is a root of all kinds of evil, and in their eagerness to be rich some have wandered away from the faith and pierced themselves with many pains. . . . As for those who in the present age are rich, command them not to be haughty, or to set their hopes on the uncertainty of riches, but rather on God who richly provides us with everything for our enjoyment. They are to do good, to be rich in good works, generous, and ready to share, thus storing up for

themselves the treasure of a good foundation for the future, so that they may take hold of the life that really is life. (1 Timothy 6:9-10, 17-19)

The Bible commands us to express careful stewardship of our wealth as one of many resources that God has given to us. It calls us to invest it in other people, thus laying up for ourselves "treasures in heaven."

Stewardship demands careful planning. If we live by conviction, we will limit what we spend on ourselves, budget our income wisely and live in order to give. More money can mean a bigger estate, vast ownership, excessive entanglement. It can also mean fruitful ministry. John Wesley made a great deal of money, but he died penniless, choosing to give all of it away. Again, the best way to use our money for service is to develop a habit of giving, to build it into our budget so that the money we invest in service is not left to spontaneous decisions at the end of the month, after our paycheck has been eaten up. The money we devote to service should be viewed on the same level as the money we set aside for house payments, food and fun.

Expertise joins money and time as the third essential element in service. It's easy to think that service is what we do when we're volunteering outside our area of expertise—we work in high finance during the week, but on Saturdays we don overalls and grab a paintbrush. There's nothing wrong with doing something different as a volunteer, but service should also tap our expertise so that it becomes an avenue and extension of what we do best.

When I worked on a Habitat for Humanity project in Chicago during my doctoral program, the project tapped the expertise of many church members. A committee of leaders organized the project. Bankers raised the money. General contractors supervised the construction. Subcontractors organized novice work crews, and skilled laborers supervised and trained those crews. Other people packed lunches, provided snacks, watched children, took photographs, cleaned up at the end of the day, scraped and painted, pounded nails, sanded floors, wired walls, stuffed insulation. Still others spoke to the community about the project, wrote articles, recruited more volunteers. The project required a broad spectrum of skills, from common laborer to money manager. Everyone was important because everyone had something to contribute.

PERSON TO PERSON

I've observed many people in the church—to say nothing of the larger community—who need to be served. They need lawns mowed, houses painted, errands run, children watched, wheelchairs pushed, books read, meals provided, appliances repaired. Over the past few months I've talked with several young widows, and their stories bear a striking resemblance. After the initial shock of the loss and a brief inundation of concern, their friends returned to life as usual and forgot about their needs. Their friends didn't realize that young widows cannot return to the same normal life. These women told me of their loneliness, of their need for a father figure for their children, of the difficulty finding good child care, of the inconvenience of doing all the household jobs themselves.

My experience as a widower was different, and I've often wondered why. Perhaps people assume that men are less capable of managing the home than women and therefore need more help. Or perhaps motherless children seem to need more nurturing than fatherless children. Whatever the reason, I received a great deal of help from my friends. One dear friend, Julie, served my family with exceptional sensitivity and consistency. She watched my preschooler five mornings a week and refused to accept payment. She picked up bulk food items for me when she was shopping at a wholesale outlet. She initiated special events like picnics in the summer. Another friend brought her two sons over to my house so all the kids could play together, and she occasionally took my daughter out to lunch.

I often asked these friends, "Why are you doing this for me?" They usually responded the same way. "I just think about my own husband in your shoes. I think about what he would have to do to maintain the home, where he would go for help, whom he would depend on. That's all it takes for me to help you as much as I can."

We will feel sympathy for widows and widowers when we think about losing our own spouse, for single parents when we think about raising children alone, for the infirm when we think about feeling forgotten and alone. Sympathy makes us sensitive to what life is like for the people who can't do what comes naturally to us. Sympathy makes us servants. It motivates us to throw our lives in with "the least of these."

Of course, any one of us can easily become the least of these. As I suddenly discovered so many years ago, what separates a happily married man from widowerhood is simply being in the wrong place at the wrong time. All of us are closer to vulnerability and neediness than we could ever imagine. What separates the competent from the disabled, the independent from the dependent, the strong from the weak has very little to do with us and everything to do with accidents of birth, place, time, opportunity and chance. There is little rhyme or reason to much of what happens in life. Servants recognize the capricious nature of life, realize that it could happen to them and throw themselves into helping the people to whom it does happen.

> *All of us are closer to vulnerability and neediness than we could ever imagine.*

ADVOCACY

Some needs require direct and personal service. Other needs demand a different strategy: advocacy. Advocacy requires servants to line up on the side of the needy and to intervene on their behalf before the people and agencies that are in a position to help.

My friend Peter works for the Mennonite Central Committee. Though involved in community organization and bureaucracy, he has never lost touch with individuals. He met Marianne on the street several years ago. Marianne, just forty-eight years old, had a college degree. But she was on the verge of homelessness, spared only by the generosity of her mother, who lived on a subsistence level herself. Marianne also had medical problems. She suffered from insulin-dependent diabetes, heart disease, liver disease, alcoholism and blindness. Despite these maladies, she was ineligible for welfare because she didn't have a medical statement certifying her inability to work.

Peter could not ignore her plight. "I raised a ruckus at the county hospital, the county welfare office, the social security office and boarding houses," he says. "Marianne and I laughed together, shared burdens together and won a few small victories. Not long after we won our biggest victory—a medical statement verifying that she was legally blind, which guaranteed that she would receive social security disability—Marianne died. The cause of her death was malnutrition and lack of medical care."

Some needs are so big that individuals cannot meet them. However willing to serve, Peter could not solve Marianne's medical or unemployment problems. Instead he served her by representing her before people in power. At such times service becomes advocacy—advocacy for minimum-wage increases, job training, health care, affordable housing, legal aid, protection of the unborn, day-care programs, nursing home improvements. Advocacy is necessary in the church, too, to draw attention to the needs of widows, the unemployed, single parents, troubled youth. Advocates function as society's conscience for the forgotten.

COMMUNITY

Peter discovered that service also requires community, because a community can look out for people in a way individuals can't. For several years Peter lived with an unusual group of ex-cons, ex-drug dealers, recovered alcoholics. They called themselves "the brotherhood," and they met every morning for prayer and Bible study. They experienced an unusual degree of mutuality, becoming like family and looking out for each other. Peter wrote:

> One morning one of the brothers shared that he was short of groceries for himself and his dependents. We left the prayer meeting and together went shopping at the grocery store. There was no feeling of someone giving and someone receiving. We knew beyond explanation that we were all equally receivers and beneficiaries. Perhaps that's why

we never said "thank you" to each other. Acts of mutual compassion were only what we were supposed to do for each other. A thank-you somehow cheapened the relationship.

Apart from community, service can become patronizing. Sleek, smooth fat cats bankroll programs for the needy and assume they have the right to control those programs; self-righteous activists think their zeal for good deeds gives them the right to impose their ideology on the people they're helping; faithful volunteers make the recipients of their service feel indebted to them and guilty if they aren't overwhelmed with gratitude. As Peter said,

> Those of us who do the serving can convince ourselves of our own self-lessness, and we can become arrogant and condescending in a pro-vider-recipient relationship. Such a relationship builds dependency, breeds resentment and continues powerlessness. This problem results because of broken community. Service within the context of commu-nity is a mutual giving and receiving as time and circumstances change.

Community links giver and receiver, forces them to see how similar they are and blurs the distinction between those who have and those who don't.

ORGANIZATION

I serve on the board of directors for the Spokane affiliate of Habitat for Humanity. We have little trouble recruiting volunteers to donate time and materials for our building projects. People welcome the opportunity to do hands-on work. We do have difficulty, however, persuading people to serve on the board. They are wary of taking ownership for the ministry, cautious about making an open-ended commitment and suspicious of in-stitutionalized forms of service. To many people service means concrete activity—pounding nails, cooking meals, visiting the sick, becoming a big brother. They don't realize that these expressions of direct and personal service require an organization to administer the program, raise money and provide training.

Americans are suspicious of institutions, and with good reason. Bureaucracies often become bloated and self-serving, consume enormous amounts of money and time to perpetuate themselves, and lose their sense of purpose. They become an obstacle to service instead of a channel for it. Many organizations—private and Christian as well as public and secular—that began with the best of intentions have become the worst offenders. Fraud, waste, greed and mismanagement disillusion the people most willing to help.

However prone to corruption, organizations are necessary if Christians want to serve on a massive scale. Mechanisms are needed to channel resources. Committees are needed to initiate and oversee ministries. Bureaucracies are needed to manage money, materials and people, whether in a local church or in a large and sophisticated organization.

Christians in America have many good organizations from which to choose. I believe that organizations such as World Vision, Compassion International, Prison Fellowship and Habitat for Humanity do a commendable job of matching resources to needs. Their overhead is low, their staff members dedicated, their vision true. They have made it possible for millions of people to do their small part in serving Christ around the world. We need more organizations like them.

SHOULD STRINGS BE ATTACHED?

The modern welfare society embodies a model of service that departs radically from earlier models. Welfare gives a handout to people in need; it does not enable them to overcome that need. It tends, therefore, to perpetuate the problem it's supposed to solve.

Service used to come with strings attached. People who needed help were required to work for it. As they received help, they learned to help themselves. The needy washed dishes, chopped wood, gleaned fields. They contributed to their redemption.

The gospel is not a message of self-help but of unmerited grace. Still, the gospel itself tells us to work out our own salvation with fear and trembling, even as it assures us that God is working in us. Self-help is good because it makes us partners with God. We can't earn our salvation. But we can grow up into it and allow God to transform us by it. However needy, people still have to realize they are accountable to God, bearers of God's image and responsible to use what God has given them as good stewards.

Habitat for Humanity is only one of many ministries that comes with strings attached. The people accepted into the program must put in five hundred hours of "sweat equity" before they can move into their home. This philosophy is based on the gleaning principle of the Old Testament, in which landowners were mandated to leave some grain in the fields after harvest so that the poor could gather it.

Other programs follow a similar philosophy. I know of churches that run programs to teach reading, to help people find jobs, to support single parents, to offer child care, to run clinics. All come with strings attached. Those strings announce that the goal of service is to help people function as productive disciples. It weans them from dependency and forces them to take responsibility for their lives.

Still, people are people. They don't always measure up to what we want them to be. They don't always turn out the way we had hoped. However much they receive, they will not always show gratitude. They might not change for the better. They might continue to drink or live in poverty or abuse their children or collect unemployment or fail to pay their bills or complain incessantly about how difficult life is.

It all comes down to motives. In our service we must remember that the needy don't owe us anything, and it's not right to make them think they do. We serve for their sake, not our own. We serve to obey God, not to get them to obey us. As my friend Peter said to me, "Service is love for our neighbors. We serve because it's right. We serve because we are being made new in Christ. We serve because it's who we are and we cannot do otherwise."

8

Encourage One Another

Therefore encourage one another and build up
each other, as indeed you are doing.

1 THESSALONIANS 5:11

Over the years many people have encouraged me, usually by writing me notes, taking me out for coffee or lunch, and surprising me with small gifts. But one person stands out. Now with the Lord, Charlotte emoted grace and sophistication. She read widely, entertained elegantly and communicated warmly with everyone she met. Never have I met anyone who encouraged people as naturally and extravagantly as Charlotte. She was especially sensitive to people in the church who do their duty without fanfare and complaint. She devoted her life to keeping them going.

Several years before she died, Charlotte let me read a note she had received from a single friend of hers who, after experiencing a painful divorce, was trying her best to raise four young children:

It's important for me to let you know that your supportive comments about my family meant a great deal to me. At this point in my life, my children consume most of my time and energy and, of course, my money! Expensive little people they are! I'm trying very hard to give them the very best start I can, and when you notice it, it means that, just maybe, I'm on the right track.

Over coffee, I once asked Charlotte to tell me the secret of her ministry of encouragement. She began by revealing bits of her past. When she was young her father invested in a farm, and the investment went bad. Though he worked hard, he never escaped the consequences of that one bad decision. "I can still see his suffering and regret," she said to me. "It lasted his whole life." That left a strong impression on Charlotte and prompted her to want to relieve such burdens in others. Charlotte experienced her own disappointments too. She never had children, though she wanted them desperately. She never attended college, though she had the intelligence and desire. She endured years of financial difficulty. But, rather than make her self-pitying, her own disappointments made her sensitive to other people and attentive to their struggles. She turned outward rather than inward. She decided to recognize and affirm people for their hard work and faithfulness when it took everything they had just to keep going.

I still remember the many warm encounters I had with this dear saint. She always looked into my eyes, held my hand and smiled gloriously. She wrote me notes, called me on the phone and invited me over for coffee. She celebrated my ministry. And not just mine either. She encouraged many people at church. "I appreciated so much your selection of the anthem this morning. It fit perfectly into the worship service." "You sang with such a peaceful countenance." "Your children look like they're doing so well right now. You're doing an excellent job of raising them." "You have used your time and talents so wisely in serving other people." "Thank you so much for helping out in this project. I don't know what we would do without people like you who volunteer for this kind of work." "Your Sunday school lesson made that story so applicable to my life." Her encouragement did wonders for me at a time I needed it. She made me want to teach better, raise my kids better, live for Christ better. Charlotte kept me going. She kept a lot of people going. We all miss her very much.

MAINTENANCE FOR WORN-OUT BELIEVERS

A society can survive only if a high percentage of its citizens live responsibly and fulfill the duties of citizenship without threat of punishment or coercion. Once that percentage begins to drop, social order comes to rely solely on the stick and the carrot. Resources are used to pressure and coerce people into obeying the laws and doing their duty. New laws have to be passed, the police force grows, courts are overwhelmed with cases, jails are overcrowded. Soon the society collapses because it can no longer rely on the majority of its citizens to abide by the law and do their duty simply because it's the right thing to do.

Like secular society, the church assumes that most of its members will live responsibly, fulfilling the basic requirements of discipleship. Some church members are here one Sunday and gone the next, unwilling to volunteer for anything because they're too busy, frequently late to meetings (if they show up at all) or inclined to jump from one church to another. The church exists for them, at least in part. But it's able to exist for them only if most of its members show up week in and week out to teach Sunday school, bake cookies, rock crying babies, run the sound system, sing in the choir, pay their tithes, show up at committee meetings, type the newsletter and visit shut-ins. The church needs a critical mass of ordinary, faithful people in order to survive. We often fail to realize how much the church depends on such faithful people until they're gone.

Encouragement is the mutuality command that meets the needs of these faithful people. Encouragement is to people in the church what maintenance is to trucks and washing machines. Toyota trucks may drive for 300,000 miles, but only if we change the oil every 3,000 miles. Maytags run well for years, but only if we take care of them properly. Their performance depends on both the quality of the product and the quality of our care. Likewise, we encourage people to keep them going as disciples of Jesus over the long haul. Encouragement is the maintenance ministry of the church.

The Greek word applies to a wide range of actions. In addition to "encourage," it can also mean "exhort" and "comfort," depending on the context. These stress the need to help fellow believers persist in faith and live as disciples. If believers flag in zeal and lose heart, we exhort them. If they struggle with a problem and stumble in their walk with God, we build them up. If they face loss and disappointment, we comfort them. There are many ways to apply this command because there are many ways our spiritual engines get run down. But the truth is one. We need encouragement when wearing out; we need maintenance to keep going.

OCCASIONS FOR ENCOURAGEMENT

We need encouragement the most when we find it most difficult to persevere—when we're distracted, busy and under pressure. The apostle Paul was aware of this need, so he encouraged believers to pray faithfully, set their minds on spiritual truths and train themselves in godliness: "Therefore, my beloved, just as you have always obeyed me, not only in my presence, but much more now in my absence, work out your own salvation with fear and trembling; for it's God who is at work in you, enabling you both to will and to work for his good pleasure" (Philippians 2:12-13).

In another letter he wrote, "Therefore, my beloved, be steadfast, immovable, always excelling in the work of the Lord, because you know that in the Lord your labor is not in vain" (1 Corinthians 15:58). The practice of spiritual discipline puts us into postures to receive the grace and love of God. Paul encouraged his fellow believers to keep up the disciplines. "Train yourself in godliness," he wrote. We too should encourage one another to pray, study, meditate, worship and seek the face of God. If we are attentive to people's need for encouragement, we will find countless opportunities to meet it, for people do need a lot of encouragement.

Sometimes we need encouragement to remain steady in difficult circumstances, such as when we face opposition and persecution, rejection and failure. I have friends who work in jobs where the atmosphere is so rabidly secular that it grinds down their spiritual zeal and confidence. Students at secular colleges take courses from professors who delight in cynicism and express hostility toward the Christian faith. Christian parents raise their children in neighborhoods where the pervasive values challenge the Christian convictions they want to nurture. Dedicated church workers try to move their church toward greater biblical fidelity, only to face opposition at every turn. All of us face the pressure of living in a fallen world that erodes faith and squelches spiritual enthusiasm. It wins more than we would like. Survival under such conditions seems victory enough.

But encouragement helps us to do more than survive. It keeps us going and growing, struggling and resisting, so that, as J. B. Phillips puts it in his translation of Romans 12:2, we do not let the world squeeze us into its mold. Encouragement enables us to stand strong and true and stable, in spite of the pressures we face.

We also need encouragement to develop Christlike character and convictions, and to grow daily in the grace of God. Encouragement helps us to be conformed to the image of Christ, who shows us what we will someday become. Hebrews 12:1-2 exhorts us to keep running the race set before us, following Christ, who for the joy set before him endured pain and suffering until he reached the prize.

PERSONAL EXAMPLE

The best way to encourage people to grow in grace is to grow in grace ourselves and set an example of faith, as Jesus himself did. Paul exhorted Timothy to set believers an example of faith, purity and righteous living. It's tough to be Christian in the modern world. We bump into many unpleasant and unhappy people—crabby, angry, ungrateful, selfish people—who make us feel peculiar just because we want to be kind and grateful. Avoiding the bad is only half of the battle. We must also embrace the good. That's the business of developing character. The best way to overcome ingratitude is by becoming grateful. The best way to overcome selfishness is by serving people. One person of Christlike character can set the pace for everyone. One person can start a chain reaction in which a growing number of people desire God and godliness.

Setting an example requires that we consider the impact of our actions and attitudes on other people. Don't be a stumbling block, Paul warned in Romans 14. We must use our freedom in Christ to build up, not tear down. We need to consider carefully what we eat, where we go for entertainment, how we talk, what we give our time to—all according to its impact on fellow believers. If something trips them up, however justified we are in doing it, we should refrain for the sake of our Christian friends. Love builds up; love removes stumbling blocks to Christian growth. (See also 1 Corinthians 8–10.)

Conversation has a peculiar power to tear down or build up. I work in an academic environment that values quickness, cleverness and humor. Colleagues and students alike win points by showing their superiority in repartee. But too often our conversations put down, intimidate and embarrass. James says the tongue holds great power. Paul cautioned believers to refrain from letting evil talk and levity come out of the mouth. People who

> *The best way to encourage people to grow in grace is to grow in grace ourselves and set an example of faith.*

want to encourage others do not put people on the defensive. They speak with goodness and grace. Their conversation creates an atmosphere of kindness and love rather than competition and cleverness.

Finally, we need encouragement to stay true to conviction when we are tempted to make small and easy compromises. Turning the steering wheel only one degree to the left or right will eventually turn the car completely around so that it's headed in the opposite direction. We need to be exhorted, or challenged—another expression of encouragement—when we gradually wander off course. Encouragement draws the best out of people. "Let's not go to that movie tonight. I read reviews of it yesterday that made me wonder if it's the kind of movie Christians ought to see." Or "Let's stop the insults for a while. I'm defensive and don't feel free to let my guard down." Or "You didn't seem prepared tonight. That's unusual for you. Is everything all right?"

I received an anonymous letter a few weeks ago, written by someone who had attended a conference I helped organize. He said he appreciated my leadership and organization. "It was one of the best conferences I've been to," he wrote. "But," he added, "I think that your humor approached being base. It was funny to most, offensive to a few. I believe that the opinions of those few matter." This exhortation nudged me to keep learning how to be a more gracious leader.

Perhaps the church would have fewer major problems if it were more attentive to the small ones. Encouragement keeps people on course before they wander too far off. It provides positive reinforcement rather than negative criticism.

ENCOURAGEMENT AS AN ART

I believe that encouragement is a medium that provides opportunity for artistic expression. Of all the commands, this one calls for careful attention to detail, elegance of style, beauty and sophistication. If done well, encouragement as an art can make people feel like they're the most extraordinary people in the world.

Of all the commands, encouragement calls for careful attention to detail, elegance of style, beauty and sophistication.

I received perhaps three thousand cards and letters after the accident that claimed my wife, mother and daughter. Some of them were works of art, masterpieces of written expression. One friend wrote at length and with deep feeling about his own divorce. Another explored the Puritan view of suffering and quoted extensively from the journal of a Puritan who had lost his wife of ten years. These letters encouraged me. I read them and reread them. I pondered every word. The people who wrote them gave extravagantly of themselves to communicate their sympathy.

These days the cell phone and computers have become the major medium of communication between friends, colleagues and lovers. Phone conversations and emails are more spontaneous and immediate than letters.

They provide an opportunity for the exchange of ideas and feelings in real time. But something is lost in this trade-off. Contrary to how we communicate by cell phone and email, letter writing pays attention to how we use words, allowing for rich and meaningful expression. People can take hours to write them or read them. They convey a kind of elegance of style and a personal touch.

Another artistic medium for encouragement is entertaining. Some people distinguish between hospitality and entertaining, as if the former embodied Christian humility and the latter secular sophistication. Perhaps the distinction is fair. Our homes should be open to people even when they're untidy, when dinner is leftovers, when toys are scattered throughout the living room. Hospitality at its best is unpretentious and natural.

Still, entertaining is also appropriate because it treats people as honored guests. I was invited recently to the home of friends—professional psychologists whose children have grown and are gone. This couple lives in a comfortable house in an upper-middle-class neighborhood in Spokane. The wife said to me in her invitation that she wanted me to join the two of them for an elegant dinner and an evening of conversation. The evening was wonderful. I felt like royalty. I was encouraged.

Good food, prepared carefully and served elegantly, has the power to bring people together. The film *Babette's Feast* tells the story of two sisters who, though beautiful and talented, choose to remain single to serve their father and his small church. After his death they take in a fugitive from Vichy France, Babette, who works as their housemaid and cook. To show her gratitude, Babette spends her entire life savings on one dinner, to which she invites the sisters and the members of the church. The meal becomes a sacramental event. Divisions are healed, relationships restored, past misdeeds forgiven. Every person around the table receives God's grace. The lavish meal serves as the medium of that grace because it's far beyond what the church members expect, deserve and understand.

One final artistic medium for encouragement is humor. Humor can be base, cutting and cruel, as all of us have witnessed too many times. Yet humor in the right setting can build people up. It can communicate affection, appreciation and respect. A friend of mine who teaches psychology at the college once sent out an announcement to his classes: "Students have until the last day of exams to pick up their brains. After that they will be donated to the theology department, which needs brains desperately." My friend actually believes that the theology department is perhaps the best on campus—which is why he dared to make that announcement. It was a subtle way of encouraging us.

Even "roasts" can make people feel significant. In fact, a roast is the ultimate compliment. It exaggerates faults, pokes fun at odd habits, draws attention to peculiarities. The assumption is that the recipient of the insults is important enough to merit outlandish attention. Roasts are reserved for those few who have endeared themselves to the many, who have served well over the long haul, who have carved out such a distinctive place for themselves that they have become irreplaceable and iconic. Such humor encourages. It tells the person that he or she has left a lasting and significant legacy.

ENCOURAGEMENT IN THE LIFE OF THE CHURCH

Churches can devote themselves to encouragement too. They can identify and honor the quiet, faithful majority who help the church fulfill its mission in the community and in the world. Too often this silent majority of people are assumed, used and neglected, while a disproportionate amount of attention is given to the few.

I know of such encouraging churches. They look for any excuse to honor each other for their faithful service, whether as custodians, nursery attendants, wedding hostesses, youth sponsors or pastors. They commission people for service before they begin teaching Sunday school, leading small groups or assuming church office. One church I know of, for example, plans two banquets every spring, one for primary and secondary Sunday school teachers, the other for adult teachers. At these banquets members of the Christian education committee express their gratitude to the teachers for their past year of service.

It takes a great deal of energy to keep a church going. Much of that energy must come from paid staff who go beyond the call of duty and from volunteers who do their duty without any financial support at all. Encouragement affirms these dedicated people for their hard work, makes their contributions known to the whole congregation and cheers them on as they try to live out their commitment to Christ at home and church, in the neighborhood and the world.

Encouraging churches don't wait for faithful people to burn out or drop out before they pay attention to them. They don't take them for granted. They help them to keep going.

ENCOURAGEMENT IN FRIENDSHIPS

I believe that the best setting for encouragement is personal friendships. Friends above all have the ability and opportunity to keep each other going. The book of Samuel tells the story of how Jonathan kept his friend David going when David was a fugitive in the wilderness and needed to be propped up. The Bible says that Jonathan "strengthened David in the Lord."

I know of a modern Jonathan-David friendship. I first met Stan and Peter when they were freshmen at the college I served as chaplain. Stan was a bright student and cocky athlete who came to college to study, play sports and party. In his first football game as a freshman he made a spectacular seventy-yard run. Stan was used to friends who maneuvered for power, mocked others with cutting comments and elevated themselves by putting others down. He expected that they would somehow disparage his first college football success, which they did. Peter, however, left a simple note on Stan's door, which read, "Great job, Stan. Nice run!" That was it. As Stan said to me, "From that day on I realized that Peter had a unique gift of building others up rather than tearing them down. He could encourage others without it being a threat to himself."

Stan and Peter soon became roommates and fast friends. They learned to be honest without being brutal, supportive without being indulgent. They kept each other on course. Peter, for example, once told Stan, who was going through a period of vocational indecision, to begin a time of daily prayer and devotion. As Stan said, this "pushed me to become what God wanted me to be. He understood that God does not call us fundamentally to do something, but rather to be someone. He always encouraged me to persevere in my faith and continue to obey God's commands."

Out of their deep friendship Stan and Peter decided to begin a ministry to the students on their wing in the residence hall. "Guys would wander into our room just to talk," Stan said. "We would listen primarily, but doors were opened to share the joy that we have in Christ. We began to work as a team. As Peter would talk, I would pray silently; as I would talk, Peter would pray. We had a common cause. We were both working to further the kingdom of God. We were bound together in Christ to serve God's purpose, not our own. This was a very big step in our friendship." The next year they started Bible studies with their friends and began to introduce them to the Christian faith. Those friends in turn began similar ministries.

Stan and Peter wanted the best for each other. They tried to help each other to hate sin, not savor it. They grew to trust each other almost completely. "I began to trust Peter's judgment about my character flaws," Stan told me. "I knew that he had my best interest in mind. I felt like my spiritual growth was as important to him as his own. He corrected me because he loved me, not because I was wrong and he was right."

After graduation, they moved to different regions of the country. For over twenty years now they have been able to see each other only twice a year, if that. But they talk on the phone once a week and have continued to deepen the friendship. "I believe God continues to shape and mold the vision of godliness he began in us in college," Stan says, "Some would say what we had during our years in college was only so much youthful idealism, and that it will fade as the realities of daily life overtake us. But I'm confident that what appeared to be idealism is really a hope in Jesus Christ for this world."

I can testify to the unusual depth of this friendship. Still, I am not convinced that it has to be so unusual. Stan and Peter's depth can be mine and yours too if we are willing to make the same basic commitment. The center of their friendship is Jesus Christ. They want to keep each other going and growing in faith. They provide each other with needed maintenance so that faith, hope and love do not wane. They have learned to encourage each other. If they can do it, so can the rest of us.

9

Comfort One Another

Praise be to the God and Father of our Lord Jesus Christ,

the Father of compassion and the God of all comfort,

who comforts us in all our troubles, so that we can comfort those

in any trouble with the comfort we ourselves have received from God.

2 CORINTHIANS 1:3-4 NIV

Sooner or later every person loses someone or something important. Every person is forced to reconsider expectations—a long and healthy life, a happy marriage, a successful career—that unfavorable circumstances dash to the ground. Grief is a school every person must enter.

Shortly after moving to Chicago, Lynda and I learned that a neighbor had lost his twenty-nine-year-old wife to a bizarre heart attack; he was left with three small children. Five years later I found myself in similar circumstances after my wife, daughter and mother were killed in a drunk-driving accident. The unexpected loss plunged me into catastrophic grief. But the loss itself was not the only problem I faced. I also inherited the pressing responsibility of being the sole parent of three young children who had their own grief to work through. I had to shop, cook, clean, pay bills, repair broken household items, visit schools, drive to activities, keep the master schedule—all without the aid of spouse or family. Busyness and exhaustion threatened to sabotage my grief by preventing me from facing the terrible darkness that my loss thrust on me.

The New Testament uses one word in particular to describe the experience of loss: *affliction*. This word describes the circumstances—trouble, distress, difficulty, suffering—that hem us in and squeeze the life out of us. The Bible teaches that affliction is inescapable, especially for Christians, who not only suffer loss like the rest of humanity but also struggle to reconcile their suffering with the sovereignty of God. Affliction symbolizes the reign of evil and death in the world. It forces a decision: to accept our mortality as final and fall into despair, or to believe there is more to life than meets the eye and that affliction will eventually give way to glory.

The apostle Paul knew something about affliction. In his second letter to the Corinthians he describes his many sufferings. He lists labors, imprisonments, beatings, whippings, dangers, deprivations, hardships and miseries. He also had to endure internal struggles. "And, besides other things, I am under daily pressure because of my anxiety for all the churches. Who is weak, and I am not weak? Who is made to stumble, and I am not indignant?" (2 Corinthians 11:23-29). Even Paul's mature faith did not spare him from suffering. If anything, his faith brought on the suffering.

THE MANY FACES OF GRIEF

My uncle John died at home in his sleep when he was in his eighties. His wife and son grieved but celebrated the many years they'd had together. His kind of death is the exception these days, even for an elderly person. More often than not people die in hospitals, engulfed by technology that makes their life—and death—appear antiseptic, cold, impersonal. Then they are whisked away and made to look "peaceful" in the casket. Death itself, even when we expect it, has become unfamiliar, distant and artificial. And that's under the best of circumstances.

Death causes grief and leaves a vacuum of loss. Even a simple and natural death causes grief that must be endured. Yet death is rarely a simple affair; it seldom happens when and how we expect. It usually finds us unprepared and unable to deal with the mess left in its wake.

For example, death can leave us with guilt, especially when it involves a broken relationship. We not only miss the loved one, we miss the chance to make it right with them. Guilt darkens our past and fills us with regret for what we cannot undo. How can we press on, burdened as we are with our mistakes? How can we redeem what has been permanently lost? How do we know we will do better the next time around?

Other kinds of death lead to what mental health professionals call "disenfranchised grief." This kind of grief remains hidden, sometimes a source of embarrassment, always a source of pain. A miscarriage can lead to this kind of grief. So can the death of a distant but significant friend or relative, the loss of a pet that functioned like a family member, or the loss of a loved one to suicide or AIDS. The loss of a "nontraditional" relationship like a live-in lover or a homosexual partner can lead to disenfranchised grief too. This grief is just as deep as any other, but it lacks the public empathy that makes the loss seem legitimate.

Death is perhaps the most catastrophic loss we face. But it's certainly not the only loss. Consider the story of Sue Ellen, a friend of mine. Sue Ellen met Matt on a blind date. He was studying to be a research scientist, she a nurse. He was a recent convert, she a lifelong Christian. After marriage their spiritual commitment cooled rapidly, and soon they dropped out of church altogether. Matt meanwhile became increasingly critical of Sue Ellen. She tried to accommodate his wishes, but the harder she tried, the more distant and sarcastic he became. His constant criticism undermined her sense of self-worth. She gained weight and plotted revenge. She also decided not to have children, since she refused to bring children into such an unhappy, tense and loveless relationship. That sacrifice compounded her grief. Sue Ellen became so desperate that she even contemplated suicide. Finally Matt filed for divorce. Sue Ellen was free of him but not free of the regret, guilt, shame, confusion and brokenness those years of marriage had caused.

People must endure other kinds of loss as well. One out of twenty-five married couples in our country cannot have children. Many of them experience a quiet grief that few people understand. So do many single men and women who want to marry but have never found a suitable spouse. Both groups may strive to change their circumstances but come up short. A close friend of mine, Rebeccah, lost her husband in a tragic accident over thirty years ago, leaving her with two young boys. She endured the terrible grief and rebuilt her life. But then she had to face another, unexpected loss. She began to realize that she might never remarry and thus never again experience the intimacy of marriage or find a father for her sons. The second loss was different from the first, but equally painful.

Church life has its own kinds of losses too. The departure of a popular pastor, the splitting of a church body, denominational controversies that polarize and embitter factions within it, theological conflicts that divide believers, and failed programs can all erode enthusiasm and commitment.

> *We have allowed differences to divide us because we have neglected to let our suffering unite us.*

They make it hard to stay true to a church body that seems to have too many unsolvable problems.

Yet grief can also serve as a catalyst to experience healing and community. Many people responded to my tragedy by telling me their own stories of suffering, which created a bond between us. For example, several months after the accident, a coach from the college approached me to express his sympathy, and we fell into a brief conversation. Suddenly he said that when he was a teenager he lost his younger brother in a drowning accident for which he was responsible. Though the tragedy happened thirty-five years ago, he wept as he talked about it. The pain was that fresh.

I am convinced that we have allowed differences in the church to divide us because we have neglected to let our common experience of suffering unite us. The gospel speaks to the broken, the weak, the lost, the lonely. It speaks to those who have suffered loss. It speaks to all of us.

A WILLINGNESS TO BE CHANGED

Grief is a solitary journey; no two people go through it the same way. Yet however unusual the grief, the comfort that grieving people desire is similar. Loss and grief provide a special opportunity for believers to show love—to strangers as well as friends, to opponents as well as allies. People suffering loss are temporarily immobilized by it, and even when they begin to function again, they find it impossible to return to their previous life. They enter a different dimension of time that distorts their understanding of the past and future. An event in the distant past, like a marriage ceremony or a baby's birth, seems like it happened yesterday, while an event that happened just a month ago seems like it occurred in another century. Everything changes. The world becomes a strange place, and they feel like strangers in it.

Good comforters must be willing to be changed by the ones who need the comfort and must be prepared to let the pain of another become their own until it transforms them. Their own world will be permanently altered by the presence of the one who suffers. It will bring detachment and superficiality to an end. It will prevent them from ever thinking again that the world is a nice place, full of nice people and nice experiences.

Time and again I have heard the same comment from my closest friends: "You have no idea, Jerry, how much your experience has changed us." They talk about the impact of my tragedy on their marriage, their children, their view of life, their schedules, their quest for meaning, their conversations late into the night. They have been changed, as they say, because they chose to get involved. They allowed my suffering to become theirs. They refused to return to their normal life after giving me an obligatory week or month. Since life could not be the same for me, they decided it wouldn't be the same for them either.

I've heard similar stories from others willing to get involved in someone else's grief, whether it was with Christian friends going through divorce, new church members working through an abusive background, or homosexuals losing family and jobs. Good comforters make room in their lives for broken people. They cook an additional meal every week for someone else; they open their home to a motherless child; they help a friend find a job; they visit shut-ins after everyone else has stopped; they set another place at the table for Sunday dinner; they listen week after week, month after month, even year after year to the same stories, the same complaints, the same problems. Comfort demands sacrificial change. If it's safe and convenient, if it's offered on one's own terms, it isn't comfort.

THE ENORMITY OF GRIEF

Good comforters encourage the grieving to face the enormity of their loss. Peter Berger uses the term *anomie*—which means literally "disorder"—to describe the effects of loss. Suddenly we find ourselves on the edge of a cliff that plunges into oblivion and we feel the ground begin to shake, realizing we are going to fall into the abyss below. Loss creates anxiety, fear and bewilderment. It is anarchic.

I liken loss to amputation—not the amputation of a limb from the body, but the amputation of the self from the self. It's the amputation of the professional self if you've lost your job. Or the husband self if you've lost your wife. Or the energetic and productive self if you've lost your health. Or the prominent leader self if you've lost your church office. It's the loss of a self you once were and knew, the self you can no longer be. I still think of myself as a husband to Lynda, as a father to Diana Jane, as a son to my mother. But the people who defined me that way, who played the role opposite me as wife, daughter and mother, are no longer there. The self I once was cries out for them, like nerves still telling me that I have a leg or an arm though only a stump remains.

Loss thus leads to a confusion of identity. We understand ourselves in large measure by the roles we play in society—husband or wife, parent or child, doctor or teacher. We experience an existential vertigo when these roles are lost. "I used to be in sales until I lost my job," a woman says to a new acquaintance. *Until I lost my job.* The words blare in her ears as she says them. She's unemployed now. She isn't what she used to be, though she still thinks of herself that way. Other words are similar. "I'm divorced." "I have a terminal illness." "I lost my husband last year." What we used to be we are no longer. We must get to know ourselves all over again under very different terms. We must discover a new identity.

Grief also plunges those who have suffered loss into deep and terrible darkness. Shortly after the accident I dreamed that I was running west toward the sun, trying to catch what was gradually slipping away over the horizon. Suddenly I stopped and glanced with foreboding over my shoulder to the vast darkness that was closing in on me. I longed to keep running after the sun because I wanted to remain in the light, though I knew it was futile. Then I realized that the quickest way to reach the sun and the light of day was to plunge into the darkness until I came to the sunrise.

Those who suffer loss must face that darkness. They must grieve. Good comforters allow them to grieve, however long and bitter the process, because they know it leads to healing. Grief is hard and long and exhausting. It's also creative and redemptive and powerful.

Since the tragedy, my capacity for pain has grown immeasurably. But so has my capacity for peace and joy. I have never felt more apathetic; I have never been so full of purpose. I have never been so tempted to hate; I have never felt such love. I have never felt so dead; I have never been more alive. I have learned that sorrow and joy, apathy and purpose, anger and love, death and life are not mutually exclusive but strangely complementary. Grief can enlarge the soul if we are willing to face loss squarely and experience its full effects. That enlargement goes both ways, since both grievers and comforters can experience the deepening of faith and growth of character that accompanies loss.

UNDERSTANDING

Those in grief welcome a visit if it comes without too many words, conversation if it comes without too much advice, an invitation if it comes without too much pressure to accept. As Sue Ellen told me after her divorce, "What comfort means to me is knowing that whoever I was talking with listened intently enough to understand what I was feeling. It's impossible to bring much comfort without knowing the situation. You can only know by listening. Understanding allows the comforter to give out more than superficial one-liners." She appreciated Christian friends in her church who offered advice only when she asked for it.

The people who were successful in giving me a sense of peace in the turmoil offered very little advice and demonstrated confidence in my decisions. At times I did ask my friends and family for advice, but I only asked people whom I knew would not be offended if I did not act on their suggestions.

Loss that involves a moral issue—a divorce, for example, or a job loss due to misconduct or incompetence—often tempts would-be comforters to make unsolicited, uninformed and unfair judgments. Sue Ellen found this form of unsolicited advice irritating, however well-intentioned. "I was not helped by the people who said hurtful things about my husband as a way of identifying and sympathizing with my bitter feelings," she says. "I had much anger and bitterness toward him, but deep within me was an amazing sense of loyalty." The people who truly comforted her did not take sides; they did not pass judgment on her husband or on her but encouraged her to live in God's grace, find healing and eventually forgive her husband.

PRACTICAL HELP

Those who have suffered loss need practical help. My friend Rebeccah, who was widowed with two young boys, was at first incapable of carrying out her many responsibilities. The meals provided by friends and relatives saw her through the first month of devastation. A neighbor took care of her boys. A good friend helped her with financial affairs. Her husband's boss spent time with her sons. Before her husband succumbed to the injuries from his accident, her pastor functioned as the hub of a complex communication network involving hospital, church and community. He also stayed with her husband during the last twenty-four hours of his life and witnessed his death in the early morning hours.

Other people who have suffered loss told me about lawns mowed, leaves raked, meals provided, plumbing problems fixed, babysitting offered, transportation and hospitality made available. Loss does not keep the lawn from growing, the bills from coming, the house from getting dirty. If anything, responsibilities often increase.

People in grief remember the number of people at the funeral. They count the cards. They treasure personal notes that bring to mind old memories of people and relationships now gone. I was thankful for the people who sent long letters months after the accident, especially a close friend who wrote me fortnightly for the first year. Other friends, a couple Lynda and I had known for years, called me every Sunday night for a year. Sometimes the conversations lasted three minutes, sometimes over an hour. They realized, as good comforters do, that grief goes on for a long time. They were willing to go through it with me without cutting off support when they thought enough time had lapsed for my recovery. Still another couple invited my children and me over for dinner every Sunday for the first year. We rarely accepted, but that did not prevent them from continuing to extend the invitation. They also decorated our home for every birthday during that first year and helped plan surprise birthday parties and other special outings.

THE FIRST DEATH IS BAD ENOUGH

Though horrific, the death that comes through the loss of spouse, friend, job, health or dream is not the worst kind of death. The worst death is that of the spirit, the death that comes through bitterness, hatred and despair. The first kind happens *to* us, the second kind happens *in* us. We bring it on ourselves. People who suffer loss are tempted to confuse the two, thinking the first causes and justifies the second. But these two deaths are not the same, however closely associated they may seem. Divorce may tempt us to hate an ex-spouse, yet the hatred is a chosen response to the divorce. The death of a child may tempt us to self-pity, yet self-pity is the result of a decision we make about the loss. Hatred, bitterness and despair will conquer and control us, but only if we allow them to. That choice will lead to the soul's death, which is worse than any other death.

Good comforters do more than understand and serve; they also caution
and challenge. They know that one death can easily lead to the second and
worse death. So they are vigilant as well as sympathetic. They challenge the
grieving to be death-hating and life-affirming.

Over the years, I have met people whose losses ennobled them, largely
because of the decisions they made in the face of loss and because of the support they received from friends in their church. I met one woman after the
accident whose simple and gracious presence made me weep, though I had
no idea why. Later I found out she had lost two children at birth and an
eleven-year-old daughter to cancer. She suffered profoundly but chose nevertheless to embrace life. She became an extraordinary human being. On the
other hand, I have also met people whose losses turned them sour. Their
presence reminded me of how important it is to choose—even in the face of
death—life and joy.

A NEW STORY

Every person imagines how life will turn out. Children daydream that one
day they will be athletes, singers on the stage, tightrope walkers, writers,
presidents, firefighters. As they become adults, this imagination does not
fade but changes, falling into line with their true goals and abilities. We like
to dream about the story of our lives. Then we try to live out that story because we want our dreams to come true.

Loss means that the dream has died, the story we imagined has ended.
Suddenly we face the difficult task of readjusting our expectations. Our
changed circumstances are not the problem; rather, the loss of the future as
we hoped for it is the problem. The loss of a future creates deep wounds in
the spirit. We think often about what would have been if the loss had not
occurred. We find it hard to give up the dream. We long to live the story that
will no longer be told.

Those who suffer loss must eventually decide to live a new story. They
must decide to readjust their plans and head into the unknown, discovering
that new story. Such a decision is frightening.

In a dream I had about a month after my loss, I was sailing a ship on a huge ocean. My three children were on board. I wanted to steer the ship back into the safe and familiar harbor I could still see behind me. But the wind wouldn't let me. So I sailed onward, into an ocean with no sign of land or ship on the horizon. I felt overwhelmed with the vastness of it all, as if I were an atom lost in infinite space. The next morning my sister reminded me in a phone conversation that the earth is round, not flat, which kept me from seeing what was ahead as I sailed my ship toward the empty horizon. I realized that in time I would discover new lands and adventures, though they were still hidden from view by the curvature of the earth. A future is there for those who grieve. But they must choose it.

A COMMUNITY OF COMFORT

Tragedy and loss have a way of unifying enemies and healing disputes. My own tragedy had a unifying impact on our church. Lynda and I were both visible people in the church. Naturally my suffering was visible too. I started to teach Sunday school again a month after the accident. The class became a community of suffering and comfort. Suddenly prochoice and prolife, Democrat and Republican, traditionalist and progressive, mission-minded and social activist found each other in brokenness—both theirs and mine. It altered the atmosphere of our public conversation without necessarily changing the opinions of the people involved. We became finite, fragile, weak people. We became more than our diverse and sometimes divisive opinions had previously allowed. We became a community of fellow sinners and sufferers who desperately need God's love and grace.

The apostle Paul understood what this suffering community could be. He wrote about it in his second letter to the Corinthians. Paul had a rocky relationship with the believers in Corinth. They had strong disagreements, as evidenced by the number of controversial subjects Paul had to address in his first letter to them. In spite of these disputes, Paul began his second letter not by disputing a point but by describing his suffering.

We do not want you to be unaware, brothers and sisters, of the affliction we experienced in Asia; for we were so utterly, unbearably
crushed that we despaired of life itself. Indeed, we felt that we had received the sentence of death so that we would rely not on ourselves
but on God who raises the dead. (2 Corinthians 1:8-9)

Paul believed that his own suffering belonged to the community of suffering. Fellow believers were given an opportunity to comfort him; he in
turn was given an opportunity to comfort them. Suffering allowed them to
recognize their need for grace and to impart God's grace to each other.

Blessed be the God and Father of our Lord Jesus Christ, the Father of
mercies and the God of all consolation, who consoles us in all our affliction, so that we may be able to console those who are in any affliction with the consolation with which we ourselves are consoled by
God. For just as the sufferings of Christ are abundant for us, so also our
consolation is abundant through Christ. If we are being afflicted, it is
for your consolation and salvation; if we are being consoled, it is for
your consolation, which you experience when you patiently endure
the same sufferings that we are also suffering. (2 Corinthians 1:3-6)

I believe that the quest for power in the church causes division; the experience of suffering creates unity. Acknowledging weakness introduces another
dimension to relationships, one transcending ideology and differences. We
come to know each other in the depths of our humanity as fragile creatures
who are subject to sickness, brokenness, grief, confusion and ultimately death.
We see each other as people with feet of clay easily toppled by life's savagery.
Even enemies can join and weep together when they discover they face another and greater enemy, their own frightening mortality. Many of our conflicts
and divisions appear trivial in the face of the terrible reality of suffering.

THE HOPE OF GLORY

Paul understood the ambivalence of faith that suffering creates. That ambivalence is resolved through Christian hope. Paul believed in the power of the gospel, but he also recognized the problem of living in a fallen world. His life experience did not always measure up to the promise of the gospel. If anything, it appeared sometimes to contradict it.

> But we have this treasure in clay jars, so that it may be made clear that this extraordinary power belongs to God and does not come from us. We are afflicted in every way, but not crushed; perplexed, but not driven to despair; persecuted, but not forsaken; struck down, but not destroyed; always carrying in the body the death of Jesus, so that the life of Jesus may also be made visible in our bodies. (2 Corinthians 4:7-10)

What made the gospel wonderful to Paul was not simply what it promised for the present, for present experience in his mind was always tinged with the reality of death, but what it promised for the future.

> So we do not lose heart. Even though our outer nature is wasting away, our inner nature is being renewed day by day. For this slight momentary affliction is preparing us for an eternal weight of glory beyond all measure, because we look not at what can be seen but at what cannot be seen; for what can be seen is temporary, but what cannot be seen is eternal. (2 Corinthians 4:16-18)

Good comforters offer hope. They keep pointing to a time when life will not be miserable anymore but will be good again, alive with meaning and purpose and joy, even if that time will not arrive until we enter eternity. They believe in the God who gives hope, and they believe for sufferers who have no hope. They carry them into the future without pushing that future on them. They let them go through the process of grief, never minimizing, never exaggerating, never trivializing. They have hope too that the process will come to an end.

The greatest hope of all, however, is the hope of the resurrection. The great enemy we face is death itself, which claims everything. In his earthly ministry Jesus performed signs and wonders. The deaf were made to hear, the blind to see, the dead to live again. Jesus' great victory, however, was not his miracles but his resurrection. The grave could not hold him. He rose to a life that would never end. The hope of the gospel is the promise that sin is forgiven, death is defeated, eternal life is ours through Jesus Christ. Easter tells us that the last chapter of God's story will be wonderful. Jesus' resurrection guarantees it.

> *Good comforters offer hope. They keep pointing to a time when life will not be miserable anymore.*

What sets the Christian community apart, therefore, is not absence of suffering but hope in suffering. We know that life has defeated death as surely as light conquers darkness. Jesus Christ is the great victor. For this reason Paul encouraged believers to press forward in humble and faithful service. "Therefore, my beloved, be steadfast, immovable, always excelling in the work of the Lord, because you know that in the Lord your labor is not in vain" (1 Corinthians 15:58). For this reason also Paul charged believers to comfort one another with the assurance that, though we grieve as the world does, we grieve in the hope that death will not have the final word—the resurrection will. As the first fruits of the new creation, Jesus has already gone before us to show us the way—to provide the way—to eternal life.

10

Bear One Another's Burdens

Bear one another's burdens, and in this way
you will fulfill the law of Christ.

<small>GALATIANS 6:2</small>

W hile speaking at a conference several years ago, I met an energetic and engaging woman, Marie, who told me her story. A mother of eight, Marie had recently lost her husband to alcoholism and was trying to survive on a small income. Though she had enough problems of her own, as she said to me, she always seemed to inherit someone else's problems too. That's exactly what happened when she met Sally.

Sally was an acquaintance of Marie's daughter. Unmarried and alone, she was searching for someone to help her through an unwanted pregnancy. She turned to Marie for support. At first Sally believed that abortion was the easiest solution, though Marie gently encouraged her to consider other options. Sally even made an appointment to visit a local abortion clinic. But when her name was called in the waiting room, she decided that abortion was no answer. Leaving the clinic, she drove at once to Marie's house and in tears asked Marie what to do. Marie had an idea. She invited Sally to move in until, as she put it, Sally could "get back on her feet." Sally lived at Marie's house for four years.

Marie redecorated a room for Sally. She helped her apply for Medicaid, arranged for her to see a Christian counselor and helped her find a job. She was Sally's coach during the delivery and sometimes cared for the baby when Sally worked. She drew Sally back into the church, where Sally became active as a Sunday school teacher and a volunteer in a crisis pregnancy program. She also introduced her to a new set of friends, one of whom eventually became her husband. She treated Sally like her own daughter.

The Bible calls what Marie did an act of bearing burdens. Her story is a moving one, complete with a happy ending. For most of us, however, it's simply too unrealistic, too impractical and, well, too radical. How many of us have ever had an opportunity to do what Marie did? How many of us want to?

Bearing burdens is inconvenient and disruptive. It requires that we be flexible, spontaneous and available. It's costly, even when we are called to do something far less sacrificial than what Marie did—though Marie refuses to label her deed as anything extraordinary. "No matter how difficult reaching out to others and carrying their burdens may seem to be," she told me, "it ceases to be a burden when the Lord turns it to love."

The Bible tells us just how costly burden bearing can be in the story of the good Samaritan. The account troubles me. For all we know, the Samaritan could have been unemployed or on vacation; he could have had time, in other words, to care for the poor man at the side of the road. The priest could have been rushing to an emergency meeting called to discuss the dangerous conditions on the Jericho road. The Levite could have been returning home to his wife and children after spending a week doing good deeds in a nearby city. We simply don't know. The story lacks that kind of mitigating detail. It's simple, direct, clear. There are no qualifications, conditions or exceptions stated. Jesus leaves us with nothing but a question and a command. He asks, "Who proved to be neighbor to the man on the side of the road?" Then he commands, "Go and do likewise."

If Jesus told a story to make the point, the apostle Paul gave a clear mandate. "Bear one another's burdens," he wrote, "and in this way you will fulfill the law of Christ" (Galatians 6:2). Like comforting, bearing burdens is a command that helps us deal with people who want to progress on the journey of faith but for some reason find it difficult. As we have already observed, to comfort fellow believers is to stop at the side of the road and stand beside them while they grieve, until they recover and resume the journey. It's not the same with people carrying heavy burdens. These people may not be able to resume the journey unless we lift them up and carry them for a while.

Although there are many social factors that make burden bearing complex, one in particular is worth mentioning. Modern psychology has given us new powers to comprehend human personhood. It has equipped us with tools to describe, diagnose and sometimes solve problems that a hundred years ago did not exist or were ignored and misunderstood. It has also given us the power to understand ourselves, especially how the past influences the present, how background, parentage and early experiences shape our identity. It provides us with knowledge to explain how we became who we are and how we developed the problems we have.

Yet in explaining the origin of our problems, therapeutic psychology can also explain them away, giving us an excuse to assign the responsibility to someone or something else. Now it's not the devil that made us do it; it's an absent father or suffocating mother or domineering teacher or mean friend or genetic predisposition. Though certainly not its intent, modern psychology has helped create a whole class of victims who can describe their problems in great detail without having to take responsibility for them. However unwittingly, modern psychology has given people the means to justify sin too, like bitterness, anger, self-pity, passivity and selfishness.

The influence of psychology in the modern world has implications for the life of the church. On the one hand, it gives us tools to help people who used to be tolerated at best, ignored or even condemned. Many churches now employ a counselor who helps people understand themselves and handle their problems and who equips members of the congregation to become a healing community for the broken people attracted to the church. On the other hand, it can create a whole new category of burdens. It's one thing when Christians have burdens that can in fact be overcome, assuming that they want to overcome them. It's another thing altogether when fellow believers have burdens to which they have become addicted. They demand much but give little in return. They share their problems but resist solutions. They use the church as a bottomless pit of love but never replenish the supply. Every Christian organization has people like this in it. It makes burden bearing itself a heavy burden.

I asked one professional people-helper, Alice, about this problem, and she agreed that it represents a formidable challenge for Christians who want to bear burdens. Alice has worked with several people who were particularly taxing. In one case she began to counsel a young woman, Lori, who struggled with depression and bulimia. Lori was a master at explaining why she had problems but was not interested in learning how to solve them. If anything, she derived pleasure in her disorders and developed a dangerous dependence on them. Alice observed, "I began to notice after several months that Lori was making no progress. Her words gave me subtle indications that perhaps she did not want to make progress. She knew how to be depressed and bulimic, and she did them well. So why change?" As Alice put it, Lori not only had burdens; she *was* a burden. The challenges presented by this kind of mentality certainly make burden bearing very complex. Still, we cannot use difficulty and complexity as an excuse. If anything, these factors demand that we look even more closely at the model laid out for us in Scripture.

In explaining the origin of our problems, modern psychology can also explain them away.

The Occasion

Burden bearing is required when Christians are unable to follow Christ in an unhindered way. When writing to the Galatians, the apostle Paul used two important words to make his point. The first word, *overtaken* ("If a man is overtaken in any trespass" Galatians 6:1 RSV), is in the passive voice, which means that it entails action being done to a person, not action a person is doing. The implication is that sin is doing the chasing and a person has been overrun by it. We don't know what conditions Paul had in mind that make believers weak and vulnerable—perhaps difficult circumstances, unanticipated problems or, as William Barclay put it, "the chances and changes of life." But we do know the effects of these circumstances on people's behavior: capitulation to sin. We have seen it too many times. People often make adversity worse by the way they respond to it.

Paul's use of the word *trespass* reinforces this idea. The Greek could be translated as "unwitting deed," "mistake," "slip." It's clearly a category of sin. But a trespass is different from willful, rebellious sin. Paul is referring to people who trip over the obstacles life puts in their way. These obstacles make them susceptible to temptation. And temptation turns into sin because of the foolish—and sinful—choices people make in response.

There are desperate people in the world—and in the church—for whom we have a special responsibility. Every day a woman like Sally discovers that she is pregnant, either against her wishes or against someone else's. Every day a young man finds out he has cancer and must decide whether it's worth it to undergo treatment that may be worse than the disease. Every day a teenage girl is mocked because she has a homely face or stringy hair or fat legs. Every day a baby is born into abject poverty and will have to grow up with none of the privileges most people in America enjoy. Every day a middle-aged woman contemplates suicide because she feels trapped in an abusive marriage or unhappy home. Every one of these people may attend a church just like ours, sit in a pew next to us, sip coffee in the fellowship hall after morning worship, participate in a small group with us. They hide their problems from us, and we hide ours from them.

Bad things often happen to decent people who do not choose these things but get their fair share anyway. Is it any wonder that so many people live in hopelessness, struggle against bitterness, wallow in depression or tremble with rage at the slightest offense? Is it any wonder that they yield so readily to sin? Sin is not justifiable. People are not merely victims. But some circumstances make sin at least understandable.

In Galatians 6 Paul commanded Christians to bear the burdens of people like that. It's a universal command, applicable for all times and to all people, because there has never been a time or place in which Christians did not have burdens. We have been out of the Garden for a long time now. Thistles, pain and death are our lot. We need help to make it on our journey to the new garden we call heaven.

THE FULFILLMENT

There is a prerequisite to fulfilling the command to bear one another's burdens. We are charged, first of all, to restore wayward Christians to a right relationship with God, and to do this work of restoration *gently,* lest we too be tempted (Galatians 6:1). Only then will we be able to bear their burdens (6:2). Not all burdens are the result of sin, but when they are, we must be courageous and compassionate enough to address it. No matter how bad the circumstances, sin cannot be excused as a justifiable response to a bad situation.

Yet sin of this kind must be dealt with gently. Paul uses the word *restore* to make the point. The Greek word can also be translated "cure," which says something about the manner with which we should confront burdened people. Paul is telling us to conduct ourselves with the same kind of kindness and sympathy as a physician displays when working with a frightened child. We are to woo them back to Christ, not yank them. Our confrontation should be padded with compassion.

Restoration implies that we help get burdened people back on their feet *spiritually.* We must deal with their sin, which is usually—though not always—part of the problem, challenge them to take responsibility for their lives and call them to repentance. We must remind them that there are ultimately no excuses for their unforgiveness, jealousy, self-pity or immorality. Even victims are free agents who have at least some power to change their lives and determine their destiny. We must help them to stand before God and become accountable for their attitude and actions. They were made in God's image. However marred that image is, vestiges of it are still there. As loving friends, we must call that image forth in them, expecting the best.

Then, as Paul says, we are ready to bear their burdens and so fulfill Christ's law of love. Paul enjoins us to stand under, hold up and carry along our brothers and sisters in Christ. At this point we must address not the sin but the circumstances that made them vulnerable to sin in the first place. We must get them back on their feet physically, emotionally, socially, economically, politically. This task may require us to help them find a place to live, get a new job, straighten out their personal finances, heal a broken relationship, build an adequate self-image, solve deep psychological problems, secure their political rights, change unjust structures, feed them healthy food, reform the criminal justice system or change bad habits.

A gospel story shows us how to proceed. The setting is important: Jesus was teaching a huge crowd of people in someone's home. When four men came, carrying a disabled friend, they could find no way to get their friend to Jesus. Their ingenuity led them to hoist their friend onto the roof, where they removed enough tiles to make a hole for the stretcher. Then they lowered the man into the middle of the room, right at the feet of Jesus. They were no doubt eager to hear those powerful words of Jesus, by this time familiar to many people, "Rise, take up your bed, and walk." But Jesus did not say those words, at least not at first. Instead, he said, "Your sins are forgiven," no doubt much to the surprise of the friends, who had sought out Jesus for a different reason. Then, when Jesus perceived that the Pharisees in the crowd were questioning how he, a human being, could presume to do something only God can do, he proved that the man's sin was in fact forgiven by showing the *effects* of forgiveness in his life. He told him to rise, take up his bed and walk.

Jesus addressed both the man's sin—the more fundamental problem—and his physical sickness—the more visible problem. It is always harder to forgive than to heal too, for sin is a more fundamental problem than sickness. Both restoration and healing are necessary, however, for wholeness.

Jesus restored the man to a right relationship with God, the prerequisite to burden bearing, and then he bore his burdens by making him well.

Bearing burdens is a mandate given to the whole Christian community, not just to a special class of professional people-helpers or an exclusive group of supersaints. Some people may devote more time to burden bearing than others; some may pursue vocations in line with burden bearing, such as counseling or social work; some may be more naturally suited by temperament, interest or skill. Nevertheless *all* Christians are called to bear the burdens of their brothers and sisters in Christ, however natural or awkward, convenient or inconvenient they find it.

Burden bearing requires a balanced strategy. First, there must be balance between individual initiative and corporate responsibility. Sometimes location, opportunity and need put a special demand on certain people to shoulder the burdens of fellow Christians. As I mentioned in an earlier chapter, three weeks after our family moved to the Chicago area we heard news that a neighbor, whom we had met only once, lost his wife to heart disease. She was twenty-nine years old and left behind three young children. A week later the grieving husband visited our home and asked if we would be willing to care for his youngest son, Mark, then three years old, while he was working. My wife, Lynda, looked after Mark for the next two years. Though we provided most of the support, many other people— friends, neighbors and especially family—helped as well. It was a ministry to which a whole community of believers contributed.

Marie's story follows a similar script. She was the one who opened her home to Sally, yet she was by no means the only person who helped get Sally back on her feet. Members of Marie's church donated a crib and baby clothes, supported Sally financially and welcomed her into the church. Men

> *Bearing burdens is a mandate given to the whole Christian community, not just professional people-helpers or an exclusive group of supersaints.*

from the church came forward to spend time with Daniel, her new son. Marie played the major role, but it was not a one-woman show. A large cast of characters played supporting roles.

And supporting roles are often as important as the leads. No Christian has everything it takes to bear all the burdens of needy Christians. We must learn to draw on the rich resources of the whole church to get the job done. Deeply troubled people need trained mental health professionals to give them good counsel; they also need ordinary friends at church who are willing to listen without comment or judgment for hours at a time. Poor people need sound service agencies to provide money, jobs and housing, but they also need friends at church to help them in little ways. Whatever our skills, connections, wealth, training or interests, we are responsible to bear burdens in the body of Christ.

Second, we must strike a balance between engagement and distance. Bearing burdens demands a sacrifice of time, money, energy. We have no choice in the matter. We do have a choice, however, in determining *how much* time, money and energy. Choices of this kind can be difficult, even torturous. Always saying no engenders guilt; never saying no leads to burnout and creates resentment.

Some people believe Jesus taught that true disciples should never set limits; it's an all-or-nothing proposition. Yet Jesus himself took time off from his ministry. He chose not to preach in some areas, and he did not heal everyone. He disappointed the crowds on more than one occasion.

It is simply impossible to bear the burdens of every person in need that we know. It is also unhealthy. For every Saturday that someone gives in volunteer service, a Saturday is taken away from family, friends and other responsibilities. For every dollar that someone donates to a worthy cause, a dollar is taken away from other causes that may not be as critical but are still important, like the church's operating budget. Granted, too many members of the body of Christ give too little of themselves or their resources to alleviate burdens in the world; their problem is indifference and selfishness. But some members give too much; their problem is busyness, distress and anxious concern.

Alice told me that she had to deal with this latter problem. Her identity was so wrapped up in helping other people that she could not set limits on her ministry. She was addicted to bearing burdens. Though she found every reason to justify her fanaticism—she was doing good, after all—she discovered in time that much of her concern for others was motivated by a need to pad her own self-image. She was afraid of disappointing people, or of being misunderstood. She needed to be needed. Alice had to learn that it is right and necessary to set limits.

All of us are responsible to shoulder burdens, but none of us is responsible to shoulder them all, and to do it alone. Sometimes we are most obedient when we say no.

Finally, there must be a balance between short-term and long-term burden bearing. Some burdens demand immediate attention from the church. People lying bloody on the side of the road require quick action; postponement may mean death. That's why we must be available and flexible if we want to fulfill this biblical command, for people in crisis cannot afford to wait for help. Yet some burdens cannot be dealt with adequately unless we devote ourselves to the task over a long period of time, perhaps a lifetime. Burden bearing of this kind isn't as spectacular and obvious, but it is certainly as important. For every wounded person lying by the side of the road who needs a good Samaritan to stop and help, there are just as many unsafe streets that need protection and unjust social structures that need transformation. For every dying cancer patient who needs immediate care from church friends, there are thousands of cancer patients who need experts in medical research to discover cures. For every victim of poverty who needs generous donations of food and clothing from Sunday morning food drives, there are cities, even whole countries, that need just laws and good government. For every person who needs a competent counselor to enable him to overcome deep personal problems, there are many ordinary Christians who need to read popular books on counseling written by professionals in the field.

Scholars holed up in libraries, executives working in board rooms, scientists sequestered in labs, politicians debating issues in legislative chambers can be burden bearers too, although the effects of their work might not be immediately evident. We must realize that our usefulness in the body of Christ is determined by how we serve Christ over the long haul. Spontaneity and availability are important qualities that must be cultivated, but they cannot replace careful study, good management, precise research, political involvement. The urgent cannot always be allowed to put off the important.

THE PERIL

The apostle Paul issued two warnings in his passage on bearing burdens. He gave the first in Galatians 6:1: "Take care that you yourselves are not tempted." We must beware that in bearing burdens we don't overestimate our own strength. None of us is invulnerable to sin—any sin, even sins that seem now to offer no attraction to us. However strong and stable we appear to be, none of us is above temptation. We should never delude ourselves into thinking that it will never happen to us, because it can.

Much of our supposed strength of faith is often the product of time, place and environment—a good background, a happy home, freedom from major problems. A change of circumstances could easily put the strongest among us flat on our spiritual back, where we would find ourselves looking up at temptations we never even imagined before. Husbands who never considered adultery have committed adultery. Women who appeared inextinguishably joyful have grown bitter. Business leaders who at one time followed the strictest moral code have cheated on their taxes. A sudden change of circumstances can throw us into a vertigo, exposing our supposed virtue for what it really is, a product of our environment.

So we must be constantly self-critical, always vigilant, never presumptuous. What separates most of us from the people who struggle with major problems is not who we are but what we have, where we live, whom we know, how we have been treated. We have the same capacity for sin as anyone.

Paul issued the second warning in Galatians 6:3-4. "All must test their own work," he wrote. The peril in this case is our tendency to overestimate—or underestimate—our own importance. The ministry of bearing burdens brings two groups of people together: relatively healthy Christians who assume the dominant and supposedly superior role, and relatively needy people who assume the subordinate and inferior role. One does the helping; the other needs the help. One is strong; the other is weak.

The first group faces the temptation of pride. They tend to inflate their sense of self-importance when they compare themselves—as they inevitably will—with those who depend on their help. They find it easy to feel like stronger and better Christians. The second group faces the opposite temptation. They tend to diminish their importance in the church when they compare themselves with those who seem to do all the giving and never seem to receive.

Not that self-evaluation is a bad thing. It comes naturally and serves a healthy purpose. The problem is that we usually use other people—their appearance, their accomplishments, their wealth, their intelligence, their personality, their interests—as the standard against which we measure ourselves and determine our self-worth. That's good news for the few people whose extraordinary gifts enable them to rise to the top. It's bad news for most people whose average abilities keep them in the middle of the pack, no matter how hard they try. Most of us will always find some people, sometimes many people, more accomplished than we are.

Paul advises us to "test our own work." We are to evaluate ourselves according to standards applicable to us alone. We must discern what God expects of us and fulfill our calling, although it might depart radically from what God expects of our friends. Common sense should convince us of the soundness of Paul's counsel. Contrary to what the Declaration of Independence says, we were not all created equal. No two of us look the same, have the same abilities, come from the same background, get the same opportunities. What is easy for one is hard for another. What is interesting to one is boring to another. We would expect a graduate student to read at least twenty-five books over a summer; we would not expect the same from a high-school dropout. We would expect a journeyman carpenter to build flawless cabinets; we would not expect the same from a novice. We would expect incredible productivity from a ten-talent person, as Jesus himself taught; we would not expect the same from a one-talent person. There are no superior or inferior people in the body of Christ, just different. God only expects that we serve him faithfully with everything we are and have.

Our inclination is to make everyone just like us. But the body is a body because it has different parts, each one with a unique function. That applies even to burden bearing. We won't always respond to a need in the same way, and we're not supposed to. We must therefore "test our own work," fulfilling our responsibilities as God has called us, neither depreciating nor inflating our work in the light of what others do.

THE GOAL

The apostle Paul concludes the passage by stating the goal of burden bearing. "For all must carry their own loads." He used the same verb as before— carry or bear—but a different noun—load. The goal of burden bearing is to enable our brothers and sisters in Christ to discover, pursue and carry out their own particular purpose in life, however burdened they have been or will continue to be. The burdens that weigh them down do not excuse them from doing their God-given duty. Thus the goal is to get them back on their feet so that they can serve God in the church and in the world.

They may not, literally speaking, have feet left to stand on. Joni Eareckson Tada, for example, suffered a serious accident when she was a teenager and has been confined to a wheelchair ever since. After the accident she became depressed and doubted the goodness of God. People bore her burdens until she got back on her feet and began to discover what God wanted her to do as a quadriplegic for the kingdom. She has had a fruitful ministry ever since, as an artist, writer, speaker, advocate. She has followed what Paul prescribed; she has learned to bear her own load.

Sometimes the "load" will correspond to the burden. Problems that have been overcome often prepare people to help others do the same. Once again, that's true for Joni, who has helped other disabled people find hope and purpose in life. That's also true for Chuck Colson, whose year in prison made him sensitive to the needs of prison inmates and led him to launch Prison Fellowship, which serves inmates and their families around the world.

Past struggles often lead people into corresponding ministries. Thus couples who have survived unfaithfulness are often the most effective in helping other couples heal broken marriages. Recovered alcoholics are often the best counselors for other alcoholics. People who have overcome the pain of abuse are often the most capable of helping the victims of abuse. If grace leads to a life of "no regrets," as Paul intimates in 2 Corinthians 7, perhaps it is in our sin and struggle that we will find our purpose in life. Old burdens will turn into blessings for the body of Christ. Our weakness will build strength into others. God will use our brokenness to bring healing to the church.

But what if people don't want to bear their own load? What if they don't want to get back on their feet? It may be necessary in such cases to forbear or serve them first. The church is not called to be like Nazi Germany, a homeland only for the strong, perfect and pure. The church was brought into being for the sake of outcasts and nobodies. Paul said it so well: "Consider your own call, brothers and sisters: not many of you were wise by human standards, not many were powerful, not many were of noble birth" (1 Corinthians 1:26). Moses told the children of Israel that God made them his people because they were inferior to the peoples surrounding them. God seems to have a special concern for people at the bottom, for the ones most easily and frequently trampled by everyone else. God is not a social Darwinist. In his kingdom the least fit survive and prosper.

Those who bear burdens should also remember that their burden bearing is ultimately a matter of obedience to God's command, not a matter of utilitarian service to others. Not everyone with burdens will respond as we would like. They might take longer to overcome their problems than we think is appropriate. They might never overcome them at all. They might even take advantage of our helpfulness, exploit our good intentions and use our resources to advance their selfish interests. Burden bearing always carries the risk of failure. Careful though we may try to be, there are no guarantees that we will be spared from being used.

We cannot allow that risk to harden our hearts to needy people. But neither should we let it make us indulgent. Foolish obedience—say, giving a dollar to an alcoholic—is not much better than no obedience at all. The best option is to obey this command intelligently. In the case of an alcoholic, the best course of action would be to buy him a loaf of bread or get him into a treatment program. As Jesus said, we must be wise as serpents and gentle as doves. Burden bearers must combine good judgment with a sympathetic attitude.

Still, the Bible charges that "all must carry their own loads." Eventually our burdened brothers and sisters in Christ should be challenged to give up the power of always being needy, to wean themselves from dependence on their problems and to become responsible before God. They must stop using past and present suffering as an excuse for irresponsibility and decide what they can do, considering their circumstances, to serve God. To do anything less is to deprive them of God's grace and strip them of human dignity.

At this point the principal problem has shifted from suffering to resistance, irresponsibility and disobedience. Sooner or later we may be forced to ask our friends the question that Jesus asked of a paraplegic: "Do you *want* to be healed?" If the answer is no, then the disease itself has become a secondary issue and their attitude the primary problem. We will need to address that attitude. Sometimes burden bearing must give way to admonition, gentle restoration to firm confrontation.

The final word in the Bible is always good news, however burdened we are. There is one burden all of us carry that no human being, save one, can bear. That's the burden of our sin. Jesus came to bear that burden for us. "Come to me, all you that are weary and are carrying heavy burdens, and I will give you rest" (Matthew 11:28). Jesus was incarnated, suffered and died on the cross to free us from a burden beyond our power or anyone else's to overcome. To rid ourselves of that burden, we must go to him.

11

Stir Up One Another

And let us consider how to provoke one another to love

and good deeds, not neglecting to meet together,

as is the habit of some, but encouraging one another,

and all the more as you see the Day approaching.

HEBREWS 10:24-25

I have been in many small groups over the years. But the most memorable and significant was a group to which I belonged during the first years of my pastoral ministry. The six of us intended to meet for six months. We met instead for over four years, every Thursday morning at six o'clock.

At first we studied a book of the Bible. We were all very pious, the group very polite. But soon we began to talk about how God wanted us to live—in our homes, at church and work, in the neighborhood. First we discussed our marriages, then friendships, then work. We expressed our deepest feelings, we revealed our weaknesses, we talked about our nagging questions. We challenged each other to become true disciples, and we discussed the struggle of trying to be true disciples. We tried to strike a balance between service in the community and commitment to family, between business at church and ministry to people, between time on the job and volunteer activities.

We became fast friends. We came to know each other well. One member of the group confessed his addiction to pornography. Another member sought our advice about buying a rundown house (the only kind he could afford) and then asked us to help him fix it up. We comforted each other during times of pain and grief. We encouraged each other when we were fatigued and lacked zeal. We had loads of fun together.

In short, we learned to obey the mutuality commands. This group, in fact, was my first foray into studying these commands in depth. We took about two months to explore six or eight of the commands that this book covers. That was over twenty-five years ago.

Intimacy in this group did not just happen. At some point each member of the group took a risk and challenged, confronted and pushed the others. Sometimes we climbed all over each other. We did not settle for anything less than the best of what each of us could be. We told Bill that he had better attend to the needs of his wife before he found himself without one. We told Aaron that his anxiety at work would not increase his income, so why continue it? They told me to cool my intensity and mitigate my drive or everyone in the church would be exhausted. The group flourished because we dared to follow the command to stir up one another to love and good works.

THE NEED TO GET MOVING

The two commands we have left to explore are what I call the *confrontational* commands. Sometimes there is a resistance to Christ that must be overcome, a resistance that requires the difficult and risky work of confrontation. I have two kinds of resistance in mind. The first is willful and rebellious; it manifests an intentional decision to disobey God's word. We will address that problem in the next chapter. The second kind of resistance is more unintentional. It is the result of inertia, a matter of natural inclination rather than defiance. It is the human condition at its unselfconscious worst. It may be the more deadly of the two simply because we are unaware of it, like death by gradual poisoning.

It should be obvious by now that the Christian life is not a journey for casual weekend strollers. It is more like a strenuous hike in the Rockies. Jesus called it "the narrow way" and warned us of its cost. He said that in the Christian life death precedes life, losing comes before gaining, renouncing the world precedes eternal life.

Many of the mutuality commands assume this tough journey. We are charged to comfort one another because life in this world is full of loss and grief. We are commanded to bear one another's burdens because circumstances often knock us off our feet. We are called to serve one another because the way of Christ exposes our desperate need. We are told to encourage one another because it is hard to keep following Christ. The Christian life seems at times to demand more than we are capable of giving.

Capable, perhaps, but not unwilling. The distinction is important. Jesus looks for intent and desire more than capability and success. What matters is that we *want* to measure up to the full stature of Christ, however far we fall short. Though desire may not eliminate our problems and get us to the goal, it nevertheless points us in the right direction and reveals the deepest longing of our hearts. It establishes a trajectory in our lives. The mutuality commands we have studied so far assume at least some openness to spiritual growth. They imply that, in spite of the difficulty, most Christians do want to make progress. They want to grow and become like Christ.

Most Christians, but not all. These final two commands deal with the "not all" people, which most of us are at least some of the time. Christians don't always want to become like Christ. Christians don't always want to pursue the highest and best to which he calls us. In these circumstances the Bible commands us to "stir up" (RSV) and "admonish" one another. We are called to "stir up" believers who suffer from inertia and need to get going again. We are commanded to "admonish" believers who are moving in the wrong direction and need to be turned around.

UNCOMFORTABLE CLAIMS

The Gospels make one point clear about Jesus' ministry. Jesus upset people. It didn't matter whether they were his followers or his opponents. His words and deeds surprised, shocked and baffled his contemporaries. The Gospel of Mark uses words like *marvel, astonish* and *fear* to describe people's reaction to Jesus. They could not figure him out. He broke their stereotypes of teacher, rabbi, Messiah and whatever else they thought Jesus was. He thought in larger categories. He had an expansive vision. He made everything in religion more extreme. He made bigger promises; he also made bigger demands. And the claims he made about himself were even bigger than both his promises and demands. This "I am," this "Son of Man," this healer and teacher, this audacious human who claimed the prerogative to forgive sins—this man promised eternal life and then demanded that people deny themselves, take up a cross and follow him.

In no book of the Bible are God's promises and demands more radical than in the book of Hebrews. It contains big promises that correspond to God's final revelation of himself in Jesus.

> Therefore he had to become like his brothers and sisters in every respect, so that he might be a merciful and faithful high priest in the service of God, to make a sacrifice of atonement for the sins of the people. Because he himself was tested by what he suffered, he is able to help those who are being tested. (Hebrews 2:17-18; see also 4:15-16)

The book of Hebrews also contains big demands. These, too, correspond to God's final revelation in Jesus. Jesus made ultimate claims; the final word has been spoken; the last and best hope has come. So we must take him very seriously. He is God become human; he is Lord. He deserves our complete submission and total obedience. No effort should be spared to do what God commands. "Take care, brothers and sisters," the author warns, "that none of you may have an evil, unbelieving heart that turns away from the living God" (Hebrews 3:12; see also 10:26).

The command to "stir up one another" is given in the context of these big promises and demands. Much is given to us; much is demanded from us. We cannot have one without the other. Observe the big promises and demands in the passage that immediately precedes this command.

Therefore, my friends, since we have confidence to enter the sanctuary by the blood of Jesus, by the new and living way that he opened for us through the curtain (that is, through his flesh), and since we have a great priest over the house of God, let us approach with a true heart in full assurance of faith, with our hearts sprinkled clean from an evil conscience and our bodies washed with pure water. Let us hold fast to the confession of our hope without wavering, for he who has promised is faithful. (Hebrews 10:19-23)

The author begins by giving two big promises. First, we can be confident of our status as children of God. Our confidence comes because Jesus has made the holy of holies accessible through his death. He has opened up a new and living way. Our status as heirs of God's total blessing is pure gift; it is given through the work of Christ on the cross. Second, we can be secure in our relationship with God. Jesus is now serving as our great high priest in heaven. He sits at the right hand of the Father, where he functions as our mediator and advocate. He is also the Father's representative before us. He is a merciful and attentive go-between, a divine ambassador who turns former enemies into friends.

But the author does not stop there. He makes two big demands as well. He tells us we must "approach" God. We must nurture our relationship with him and never presume on his kindness by thinking his promises release us from the responsibility to seek him with heart, soul, mind and strength. God must be our goal, our passion. We must be single-mindedly devoted to him and pursue him as life itself. We must also "hold fast to the confession of our hope without wavering." We must persist in faith, endure when times are tough, hold on when everything around us screams that God is distant, that faith is futile, that prayer is empty, that worship is a sham.

It's not easy to believe God's big promises, not easy to meet God's big demands. That's why the author of Hebrews tells us "to stir up one another." "Let us consider how to stir up one another to love and good works, not neglecting to meet together, as is the habit of some, but encouraging one another, and all the more as you see the Day drawing near" (Hebrews 10:24-25 RSV). God's promises seem almost too grandiose to believe, his demands too difficult to fulfill. We can't believe alone, and we can't obey alone. In the Christian faith, no one dare journey alone.

THE COMFORT ZONE

Faith and obedience come hard because of doubt, struggle, temptation, exhaustion and busyness. Yet in my mind these difficulties are not the greatest obstacle in the Christian life, however prevalent they are. The greatest obstacle is more subtle, which is why the Bible warns us against it so strongly. Scripture calls this problem "lukewarmness." I call it inertia.

Inertia in the Christian life is dangerous because it seems so natural and justifiable. It's like water that flows to the lowest elevation possible, where it can rest after cascading down mountainsides. People have a natural inclination to seek that same state of rest and ease. We like things to be convenient and controllable, stable and predictable. We want "givens" because they provide security. Consequently, we fall into predictable behavioral patterns—in private life, in relationships and in society. Inevitably free choices become necessities, spontaneous activities become habits, innovations become traditions. Bold action sooner or later turns into "the same old thing." We like to settle into a routine. Rushing rivers always empty into placid lakes. We tend toward inertia.

Take personal habits. Most people get up at the same time, dress in the same clothes, eat the same breakfast, work at the same jobs, pursue the same interests outside of work. We are creatures of habit. Marital roles follow the same rule. Husbands and wives fulfill different roles. One takes out the garbage, the other does the dishes. One cares for the children, the other puts bread on the table. One coaches soccer, the other handles music lessons. Perhaps they divide responsibilities evenly; perhaps one does much more than the other. Regardless, each fulfills a different role.

Groups demonstrate the same tendency toward predictability and stability too. In my work as a professor on a small college campus, I frequently

Stir Up One Another   151

observe student behavior outside my office window. I watch the same herds of students move toward the dining hall at about 5:15 every afternoon. I see those same groups frolic on the lawn in the fall and act out rites of courtship every spring. Students could turn the tables—as I'm sure many do—by noting the predictable social patterns that faculty follow.

Imagine what life would be like if we didn't fall into habits, fulfill roles and obey rules. It would be unstable, uncomfortable and inefficient. It would require an enormous amount of energy because we would never know what to expect from day to day. Life is built on habit, order, routine, role, responsibility. Without predictable patterns we would live in chaos and anxiety. We assume—rightly so—that life tomorrow will be roughly similar to life today and yesterday. We depend on routine as much as we depend on the sun coming up.

Stability and predictability cost us something. The cost is sameness, blandness, boredom and sometimes injustice.

Yet stability and predictability cost us something. The cost is sameness, blandness, boredom and sometimes injustice. There is nothing wrong with following a set schedule from day to day. But what happens when that schedule keeps us from enlarging our world with new experiences or challenges? There is nothing wrong with fulfilling different marital roles. Yet those roles might be unfair when children come, the husband goes back to school or the wife gets a new job. There is nothing wrong with policies that make institutions run more efficiently. Yet sometimes rules made for the sake of efficiency and productivity stifle creativity; rules made to give the most experienced people authority may give way to an "old-boy network" that keeps new blood from rising to the top.

This is also true in the Christian life and the church. We need and desire stability. We like things predictable. Routine helps define who we are. For example, a habit of daily devotions nurtures faith. I have a friend who has read through the Bible once a year for twenty years. That habit has built personal discipline, expanded his knowledge of Scripture, deepened his love for God. Likewise, traditions in the community of faith give us a sense of identity and continuity. I for one like familiar liturgy, older hymns, a printed prayer book. A set church schedule helps us order our week around spiritual activities. We can look forward to Sunday worship, a midweek educational program, a morning Bible study, an important committee meeting.

Still, a routine poses the risk that personal devotions will grow stale, worship dull and lifeless, a small group ingrown and exclusive, the church inflexibly tied to forms that fail to adjust to cultural changes. I know of people who gave sacrificially to the church during their early years of marriage but have not increased their tithe since then, even though their income has tripled. Their giving may be predictable; I'm not sure that it's right. I know of churches that have worshiped the same way for twenty-five years; they minister meaningfully to the people who are familiar with the liturgy but ignore the needs of secular outsiders uncomfortable with such formality. I know of denominations that have defended their institutions and traditions at the expense of outreach and evangelism.

This is the problem of living in the comfort zone. Comfort zone Christianity appeals powerfully to certain legitimate impulses within us. But it is still dangerous. It can lead to laziness of spirit, deadness of faith, a routine that gives the appearance of religion without cultivating a heart for God. It makes us nice, decent and respectable. It can also lead to dead worship, exclusive churches, lifeless devotions, token service, easy giving, superficial knowledge of the Bible. It is, as the Bible calls it, lukewarmness, which is more perilous than open rebellion (Revelation 3).

Jesus said that the new wine of his message and ministry—the new wine of the gospel—must be poured into new wineskins. The old wineskins cannot contain the radical power, energy and vitality—the big promises and big demands—of the gospel, which will burst them. We cannot therefore maintain habits if they keep us from drinking the new wine of Jesus! We must be flexible, eager to change.

BEYOND THE COMFORT ZONE

The mutuality command "Consider how to stir up one another to love and good works" is intended to push Christians beyond the comfort zone. Outlined in the biblical command are five steps that must be taken to obey this command.

The first step is *concentration*. We must consider *how to* stir up. The Greek word used here means "to take notice of," "observe carefully," "contemplate," "fix the eyes of the spirit on." It's the kind of word that describes how an artist gazes at a subject, how a surgeon studies an x-ray, how a scholar combs through data, how two lovers look at each other.

Concentration implies that we think carefully and creatively about the needs of the people in our churches. It requires us to tailor general principles of Christian living to fit individuals whose background and experiences differ as much as the appearance of their faces. We must discern how to apply this command uniquely to each individual in our circle of friends at church. One may need to change careers, another to remain in a job that she would love to leave. One may need to join a small group, another to quit one. One may need to memorize the book of Colossians, another to pray the "Jesus Prayer" one thousand times a day.

I know of someone who keeps a section in his journal on the needs of his family and friends. As he prays for them he jots down ideas and insights. He may think of a gift for his daughter's birthday months away; he writes the idea down so that he can surprise her with a special gift when her birthday arrives. He may observe a defect in his son's personality; he reflects on that insight in his journal so that, at the proper time, he can talk thoughtfully about it with his son. He may spot an unusual talent in a friend; he records those observations so that down the line he can affirm that gift. He is mastering the first step of this command. He is learning to concentrate on the needs of others.

The second step involves *strategy*. It's not enough to think about our friends' needs, we must also think about how they can grow. We must be deliberate. We must come up with specific plans and outline possible steps of action. It's one thing to think about a friend's need to master the basics of Christianity; it's another thing to give him two good books on Christian discipleship and propose reading them together. It's one thing to believe that your church needs deeper fellowship; it's another to go away for a Saturday with twenty key members to design a program to revitalize small groups. Christian faith flounders when we talk endlessly in generalities and neglect to turn our ideas into a specific course of action. We obey this command when we develop a concrete strategy: start a soup kitchen, write letters for Bread for the World, initiate an evangelistic Bible study in our neighborhood, start a second worship service, attend a marriage renewal seminar.

The third step calls for *action*. In the Greek language the word was used originally to describe the effects of a high fever. It leads to paroxysm, frenzy, delirium. The New Testament applies the term to how people influence each other, whether for good or for evil. It's possible to "stir up" one another through irritation, disagreement or manipulation. But it's also possible to "stir up" one another through inspiration, challenge and example. In either case, the word conveys the idea of a feverish activity. This command demands energetic, creative action.

The fourth step sends us in a specific *direction*. We must consider how to stir up to love and good works. In other words, we must care about people and important causes. People are important to God. God wants us to treat people as ends rather than as means. Years ago I memorized 1 Corinthians 13. Every so often I review that chapter and evaluate my life in its light. I always come to the same conclusion: I am ashamed at how loveless I am. I can point to many accomplishments; I have developed many competencies over the years. I have pursued many interests and hobbies. But I question how well I have learned to love.

Love, of course, is what people are crying for in our culture—church people, neighbors, family members, colleagues. They must be our supreme concern in life, not (taking my own interests as an example) reading good books, building furniture, following the Mariners, tending my garden, camping and backpacking, writing and teaching new courses. Jesus commands us to love God and neighbor even above ourselves.

One way we love people is by investing in causes that meet their needs. Christians are not wanting for good causes these days. I receive probably five hundred letters or emails a year from Christian organizations that represent some great cause. I can't embrace them all, but I can embrace one or two. Recently I met a man who, upon his retirement, sold his home and now pulls a trailer around the country to communities where he can help build churches. I know a physician who travels to Latin America one month a year to provide free medical care to villages. Never before has the church had so many opportunities to serve human need. What is lacking is not the causes but the willingness to give our time and energy to them.

The final step centers on the need for *support*—not neglecting to meet together. Christians can't stir up one another if they never see each other. There must be consistent participation, regular attendance. That standard presents a difficulty for people who live in a highly mobile, leisure-oriented society. Many churches virtually shut down during summer because so many members leave for vacations or spend time at cabins and cottages. Sometimes it's not much better during the other nine months. This lack of commitment kills momentum and undermines continuity. Sunday school teachers have difficulty building on what they taught the week before. Choir directors can't introduce new and challenging music. Small groups flounder. Ministries to needy people die. How can a church grow in numbers and depth if over half of its membership is hit-or-miss?

OBEYING THE COMMAND TO STIR UP

The Bible contains many examples of stirring up. Mordecai stirred up Esther to courageous action when he said, "Perhaps you were brought into the kingdom for such a time as this." The apostle Paul stirred up Philemon to care for his runaway slave. The author of Revelation stirred up the seven churches to faithfulness and service during a period of intense persecution. These biblical illustrations are useful examples of how to obey this command.

I know one pastor who learned to stir up a declining congregation. The church was quite ordinary, similar to most congregations in America. It wasn't located in a growing community and didn't have lavish facilities or a perfect location. It wasn't a new congregation, loaded with money and professional people. Yet it's unusual because it has carved out a fruitful ministry in a depressed neighborhood after enduring a precipitous decline throughout the 1960s.

At that time Case Boersma accepted a call to the church as pastor. I know Case well, and he is exceptionally good at stirring up. He has a simple and clear theology of renewal, and he has applied this theology to the church for over thirty years. "Stirring up," he wrote to me, "demands an ethos and atmosphere of grace. Grace keeps a church from falling into the traps of reductionism and works righteousness." The first business of the church, he says, is to "create a womb of grace where healing and hope can abound." Without this womb, the process of stirring up leads only to further despair and greater complacency. The key to creating this womb is unconditional love, embodied in the work of Christ on the cross.

Stirring up a congregation to love and good works leads to a kind of death—the death of the familiar, of attachment to the past, of control and power. Case realized soon after arriving at the church that, for the church to change, it would have to go through grief:

> Change invariably leads to loss, loss to grief, grief to anxiety and, finally, anxiety to hostility. We need, therefore, to acknowledge grief. We need to understand and choose to walk with the grieving. We need to lift up the truth that God calls us to change. We are pilgrims on the move and not settlers in the parlor. As I reflect back, I can recall sharing new ideas and watching, feeling and sensing the pillars of the church react with fear. It was my goal to listen to them, encourage and affirm them.

Yet Case did not shrink from challenging the church to move forward. He kept holding up a vision of what the church could become. "People become 'stirred up' when they see a vision that the Holy Spirit was birthed and inspired," he says. "This vision needs to be something larger than they are." Case advocated the practice of "writing new chapters" every three years so that the church would develop a sense of history and see the progress they had made. "The Spirit causes new needs to be recognized, new programs to be developed, new approaches to meet the needs of the hurting."

The church witnessed major changes during those thirty years. It transformed its image of itself, expanded the staff, intensified ministry to youth and family, and initiated a ministry to the Latino population. It also deepened its prayer life, enlarged its music ministry and renovated the sanctuary. It is now starting cell churches. It developed programs to meet the community's needs.

Stirring up a congregation to love and good works leads to a kind of death— the death of the familiar, of attachment to the past, of control and power.

Case has called the people to prayer and praise. He confesses that without these spiritual disciplines, the life of his congregation would wither, however busy it would appear to be in running its many programs. In his mind it's not enough for the people to do the work of God; they must also *be* the people of God and practice the presence of God.

> When God's glory is revealed to his people, they are "stirred up" by his majesty, love, power and presence. Our Saturday evening prayer service, our Sunday evening praise service, and the emphasis on prayer in all musical endeavors have been pivotal in the "success" our church has known recently. We find that God's Spirit is released through contemplative prayer. The inner person is recreated. This enables us to love and serve again, joyfully.

Case Boersma is a master at affirming members of the congregation for their faithful service, and he draws attention to them so that others have examples to follow. At the same time he is sensitive to people who feel left behind and left out. He spends a great deal of time listening to angry, disappointed, frustrated and critical individuals. But he does not allow such negativity to keep him from nudging the congregation forward.

During his first five years at the church, Case emphasized hope and vision—hope that the church had a bright future, vision that it could reach outsiders. He began to outline a strategy for renewal. He preached on it frequently, reviewed it monthly at the elders' meeting, and mentioned it at Bible studies, church potlucks and informal coffees. He dealt with the grief and absorbed the criticism, but he would not let up on the pressure. When the church began to grow he added staff, printed a weekly newsletter and started new programs. Above all, he and his family gave of themselves; they were visible, energetic, encouraging, joyful. The church reversed the decline, added new members and reached out to the community. Members became proud to be part of the church, eager to support new programs and willing to invite their friends. The church eventually became a dominant institution in the community.

CONTINUITY AND CHANGE

The church Case Boersma serves is dramatically different now; yet people who have been gone for many years and returned to visit mention continuities as well as changes. They say that the old church is still somehow there—the leadership is largely the same; the order of worship is the same, as are the church's location and facilities. The church is characterized by the same faces and the same "feel." The changes are significant, but not so radical that the church of the present is a stranger to the church of the past. It has undergone several radical surgeries, yet the body is the same.

This sense of continuity with the past should put our minds at ease. Stirring up is best undertaken by appealing to our best self in Christ, to the best church or institution that lies latent under the surface. Lutheran churches don't have to become Baptist to be renewed; they just have to figure out how to become better Lutheran churches. Small churches don't have to become megachurches to minister fruitfully in the name of Christ; they just have to discern how they can serve Christ as small churches. Liturgical churches don't have to throw out tradition or their stained-glass windows to make worship lively; they just have to reinvigorate their liturgy.

What is true for churches is also true for individuals. Quiet and sensitive people don't have to become noisy and aggressive; activists don't have to become contemplatives; scholars don't have to become popularizers. Stirring up means we become all God meant us to be. It's not helpful or possible to stir up people to something they are not and can't be. It's not right to stir up a church to change so much that it becomes unfamiliar with the church it once was. Stirring up preserves the best of what we already are, the best of the tradition our church embodies. Continuity and change are partners, not enemies.

Both are important. Change pushes us beyond the comfort zone; continuity keeps us from forsaking the usable past. We need discernment to shape our vision of what stirring up requires, both for our friends and for our churches. The fact that daily devotions become routine does not mean that, in the name of renewal, we should reject that discipline. The fact that liturgy can degenerate into dead formality does not mean that liturgy itself is bad. Volunteer service that has become methodical and wearisome does not give us an excuse to give all of our time to contemplative prayer and meditation.

Sadly, much of church history can be summed up in its reaction to what went before. When a religious tradition goes bad, a new movement may reject it entirely; soon that new movement becomes a tradition and over time it too goes bad. Another movement emerges and reacts against it, and so the cycle repeats itself endlessly. The secret of stirring up is *balance*—to push people, churches and Christian institutions beyond the comfort zone without breaking continuity with the past. Balance requires us to expand our vision of discipleship, not change it entirely; to enlarge our capacity to know and obey God, not swing periodically from one extreme to the other.

12

Admonish One Another

Let the word of Christ dwell in you richly;

teach and admonish one another in all wisdom;

and with gratitude in your hearts sing

psalms, hymns, and spiritual songs to God.

COLOSSIANS 3:16

Admonition is the mutuality command we obey least often, and when we attempt to obey it, we usually do the worst job. Admonition seems awkward and contrary to our basic nature, like throwing a baseball with the opposite hand. Still, it's a biblical command. In fact, it's mentioned more often than nearly all the other mutuality commands. Perhaps, as we shall see, for good reason.

We hesitate to admonish for many reasons. For one, we feel unqualified and unworthy to admonish. "Who am I to tell him to change? I've got enough problems of my own!" We have a fear of being judgmental and intolerant, of picking the splinter out of someone else's eye before removing the log from our own. The truth is, awareness of our own shortcomings may keep us from obeying this command at just the point we are most able to do it well.

There is another reason we fail to obey this command. We feel relief and a sense of camaraderie with people who have weaknesses similar to ours. We think to ourselves, "Well, at least I'm not the only one who has that problem!" I have three delightful children who happen to be very spirited. As adults, that spiritedness has served them well. They take the initiative; they dare to try new things. But as kids growing up, that spiritedness posed problems. Everyone else's children seemed well-behaved in comparison. *Their* kids never ran around after church like mine did. Their kids never whined and cried. *Their* kids never fought. Then suddenly I would see a brother pop his sister on the head, a six-year-old scream uncontrollably, a ten-year-old mouth off to her father. In that moment I realize that I wasn't alone anymore, that my friends, who seemed to be normal and healthy Christians, still struggled to be good parents, that their children were imperfect. That knowledge comforted me.

We would rather keep the peace than deal with a strained relationship, hurt feelings, misunderstanding or anger.

Perhaps the most common cause of our failure to admonish is adaptability. We have an amazing capacity to adapt to people we know well, to tolerate idiosyncrasies and accept them even when they're at their worst. We tell ourselves love is the reason for this. But more often it's because we realize—perhaps unconsciously—that the cost of admonition is too high. We would rather keep the peace than deal with a strained relationship, hurt feelings, misunderstanding or anger. This is why some wives tolerate their husbands' irresponsibility, rudeness and selfishness, why some churches remain loyal to a pastor who's not doing the job, or why friends overlook, even chuckle affectionately at, obnoxious behavior in a neighbor.

We also hesitate to admonish for another reason—a reason that reveals the wickedness of the human heart. We derive pleasure in spotting weaknesses in others, especially our Christian "enemies," and we like to tell our friends about them. We prefer gossip to admonition. This habit is common among Christians because we can couch our gossip in such pious language.

"Please pray for her," we say after having already said too much.

Despite all these difficulties surrounding admonition, no excuse is good enough to excuse us from the obligation to obey this command. We are responsible for one another. That's the simple and frightening truth. We might not believe it; we might not accept it. But we cannot change it. What I become depends on how my Christian friends respond to me when I'm at my worst. The same holds true for them. And God will judge us for it. The prophecies of Ezekiel (for example, in Ezekiel 33) contain sober warnings aimed at those who disclaim responsibility for others—we are their "watchmen." We are responsible to warn them about their sin. If we neglect this duty we will also be held responsible for their disobedience.

Admonition makes good sense once we consider the nature of discipleship. It's a steep, rugged, narrow path. A tough path requires a tough faith; tough faith requires tough love; tough love requires that we show concern for people in a variety of ways: encouragement, comfort, service, forgiveness. And admonition.

The question, therefore, is not whether we should admonish but how. We must learn to do it well.

THE MEANING

The Greek word for *admonish* means to "set right, correct, warn, lay on the heart of someone." It denotes confrontation, challenge, correction. Behind it lies the assumption that something is very wrong with that person's life.

If comforting requires that we stop at the side of the road to be with grieving people, if bearing burdens requires that we get people back on their feet again so, if stirring up requires that we get inert Christians moving, then admonition demands that we turn disobedient Christians around. We see what will happen if they do not. Appealing to their conscience, we challenge them to make a choice. "Here are the alternatives: your way or God's way. Which shall it be?"

Admonition often has a harsh edge to it. In Scripture, the prophet Nathan says to King David, "You are the man!" (2 Samuel 12:7). Jesus addresses Simon Peter, "Get behind me, Satan!" (Matthew 16:23). Paul instructs the Corinthians, who had someone in the church practicing sexual immorality, "to hand this man over to Satan for the destruction of the flesh, so that his spirit may be saved" (1 Corinthians 5:5). As these references indicate, admonition is not something Christians welcome. It's therefore important that we welcome, encourage and forbear first, to accept and affirm them before we challenge them to change.

Admonition can never be used as an excuse to clobber a friend because she does not measure up to what we think she should be. It does not give us license to lord it over others. First we must listen, sympathize and affirm. Then we ask, "Is anything hindering my friends from growing in Christ? Are they wandering off course?"

Those questions are critical. While we should forbear always, we should admonish seldom. In many cases the problems we see are not the result of defiance but of weakness. Time and experience will correct most of them. We don't take an eight-year-old to the doctor because he isn't five feet tall yet. We take him to the doctor if something is hindering his growth, if he is not growing as an eight-year-old should. People need room to grow into Christlikeness, and admonition is reserved for those few cases when something is keeping them from growing. It corrects a course, challenges a problem, confronts resistance to God's Word. It addresses attitudes and behaviors that impede growth.

Before we admonish, therefore, it's important to understand the basic nature of people. There is a difference between a person's unique personality and a perversion of personality that results from disobedience to God's commands. The former requires the development of character, which enriches personality; the latter requires admonition so that Christian growth can be resumed.

Take a busy, active, productive church member. She's always the one to volunteer for responsibilities, and she always gets the job done well and on time. Yet lately we've noticed that she has become frantic, nervous. She arrives late and unprepared to meetings; she's doing her work poorly. She

seems to be neglecting her inner life and lacks serenity. It's time for admonition. "I've always admired your energy and commitment, but recently . . ."

Or take a naturally affectionate person. He loves to embrace friends, male
and female alike. He's emotional and demonstrative. We appreciate his out-
going personality, his expressiveness. But lately we've observed that he's
sending a skewed signal to several women at the church. Others have noticed it too. The time has come for admonition. "I've always enjoyed your
warmth and affection, but I've observed lately that . . ."

The point is, we should not admonish Christians for their idiosyncrasies
and imperfections. If we did, we would be admonishing all day long. It
would become a wearisome, oppressive business. Admonition should be reserved for problems that prevent Christian growth, not problems that normal Christian growth will solve. Thus we should not admonish serious people unless they become excessively self-serious. We should not admonish
spontaneous people unless they become consistently irresponsible. We
should not admonish disciplined people unless they become inflexible and
fanatic. We should not admonish conservative people unless they turn negative, critical and self-righteous. Admonition requires discernment. "Who is
this person?" we should ask. "Is she heading in the right direction or is she
wandering off course?"

Admonition is best practiced early on, at the beginning stages when a wrong
course has been set but the consequences have yet to be experienced. It should
not be reserved—as it often is—for big, juicy, scandalous sins that titillate us
and make for delicious tidbits of gossip. I have heard horror stories about unmarried couples who've been dragged before their entire congregation to confess fornication after the woman had become pregnant. I do not deny the sin.
But how much good is accomplished by this humiliation? The proper time for
admonition is not after the woman is pregnant but before, when the couple is
experimenting with sex but unaware of the physical and spiritual consequences. If anything, admonition should be leveled at the church family that
sits there gawking, snickering and shaking their heads. The sin that needs exposure at that point is not fornication but hypocrisy and judgment.

Admonition, in short, does not wait for the consequences of sin to become apparent before it goes to work. It challenges lust before it turns to adultery, greed before it eases into materialism, little lies before they grow into big ones, factionalism before it causes a church to split.

THE ACT OF ADMONITION

Jesus outlined how we should address offenses in the church that call for admonition.

> If another member of the church sins against you, go and point out the fault when the two of you are alone. If the member listens to you, you have regained that one. But if you are not listened to, take one or two others along with you, so that every word may be confirmed by the evidence of two or three witnesses. If the member refuses to listen to them, tell it to the church; and if the offender refuses to listen even to the church, let such a one be to you as a Gentile and a tax collector. Truly I tell you, whatever you bind on earth will be bound in heaven, and whatever you loose on earth will be loosed in heaven. Again, truly I tell you, if two of you agree on earth about anything you ask, it will be done for you by my Father in heaven. For where two or three are gathered in my name, I am there among them. (Matthew 18:15-20)

What can we learn from this passage? First, admonition is best done privately; involving no one but the offender and confronter, which will build trust and eliminates the nasty complications that arise when people far removed from the problem get involved. Too much talk spoken by too many people who have too many opinions undermines the work of admonition. It makes it difficult for a person, already cautious and resistant, to change when he discovers that uncommitted, uninformed and unloving people have heard what should have been kept private.

In my mind we have too many conversations in the church about other people's problems. We like to be insiders and know everyone's business, especially when we're not required to do anything about it. Admonition requires that we deal directly with people. We must "speak the truth in love" to the only person who needs to hear the truth, the only person who can do something about it. Admonition goes public only when, as Jesus intimated, there is a hostile response. And by public I mean to people of experience, wisdom and authority—the elders of the church—who are in a position to deal firmly and redemptively with the problem. Then, only after every option has been exhausted, should the offender be asked to leave the church.

The danger with admonition is that it can turn into a power struggle. The admonisher goes public before the proper time, demonstrating that she wants power. The admonished becomes angry and defensive.

Privacy transforms the dynamic. The confronted person does not feel the urge to defend himself before the entire community. Repentance does not spell defeat. There is no sense of "You lost, I won" or "I told you so." Privacy keeps power from becoming the central issue; it draws attention to what matters most—the need to repent and make one's life right with God.

Second, admonition is best done positively. The purpose is, as Jesus taught, to "regain" a brother or sister. Admonition does more than put down; it also builds up. It aims at restoring, making right, solving the problem. Criticism of weaknesses is easy; building strength is difficult. Telling a friend she must break off an affair is one thing; helping her rebuild a marriage is another. Harping on someone's need to lose weight is one thing; helping him change his eating habits is another. Admonition demands a long-term commitment to see our friends through to repentance, recovery, restoration. As Jesus said, we want to "regain," not simply reprove.

I asked Doug, an academic dean at a Christian liberal arts college, to reflect on his experience with admonition as a longtime Christian leader. In a letter to me he remembered two critics from his past who both admonished him. "My first critic," he wrote, "accurately assessed my shortcomings, my need for growth."

I couldn't argue with his evaluation, but I bristled when I heard it. What was all wrong was the spirit in which he offered his criticism. It was a judgmental spirit. From his perch of superiority, he verbally beat me with a catalogue of how I failed to measure up to accepted standards of performance. And, of course, he was right. I had failed to measure up. But his insistence on putting me down instead of building me up only made me defensive. He hadn't earned the privilege of being my critic.

The second critic, Doug continued, communicated a different spirit. He had the rare ability to be "both critical and kind at the same time."

I never perceived my second critic as a critic. I perceived him as a caring friend. His was a spirit of helpfulness and kindness. I knew that he cared enough about me to want me to grow. And so I didn't bristle at his suggestions for growth, his criticisms. I even sought them out. He helped me immensely, not with a spirit of superiority, but with the humility of a fellow Christian pilgrim who acknowledged his own need to grow. He had earned the privilege of being my critic by first being my friend.

This kind of positive admonition appeals directly to the conscience. It does more than prove and argue; it convicts. It appeals to the highest and truest self in a Christian, the self that's being shaped into the image of Christ. It asks, "Is this what God wants for you? Is this how God intended life to be lived? Is being right worth it when you consider the price you are paying?" Admonition summons people to Jesus Christ, to repentance and forgiveness, to death and resurrection. It calls people to spiritual transformation. That's the most positive message we can possibly give.

Third, admonition is best done prayerfully. Admonition is risky business. There is no guarantee that our friends will welcome our admonitions, repent of their sin and set a different course. They might take offense, reject our pleas, cool to our friendship. They may even rally a group of sympathetic friends around their cause. The apostle Paul understood the risks. On more than one occasion his admonitions were not received enthusiastically. His first letter to the Corinthians, for example, was dismissed by some members of the church. They challenged his authority and continued to tolerate ungodly behavior and believe false doctrine. So Paul had to write what some scholars call "the severe letter" to expose their sin. So anxious was he over their response to this letter, now lost to us, that he could not even preach. He wanted to know the outcome to this painful dispute.

Prayer greases a tense situation, prepares the heart (both theirs and ours), softens the will. Prayer sends the Holy Spirit ahead of us so that the most important work—making someone open to God—is already done before the admonition is given. Prayer protects us from the presumption of thinking that our words are enough and keeps us from overestimating our own powers. The deepest parts of people are beyond our reach. Only God can touch those deep parts. Prayer invites him to.

OFFENSES NEEDING ADMONITION

The church is divided, perhaps more deeply now than ever, over what problems require admonition. Admonition implies standards. Standards imply rights and wrongs. What constitutes right and wrong is presently up for grabs. Such confusion makes admonition difficult. How can we obey this command if it's impossible to agree on basic doctrinal and moral standards?

Christianity is a religion of the book. So what does the Bible teach? What beliefs and behaviors did the authors single out for admonition? I believe that these can be broken down into three categories. The first involves theological problems, the most important of which is our view of Jesus Christ, or what theologians call our Christology. The New Testament proclaims that God came to earth in the person of Jesus Christ, who was perfectly divine and perfectly human. This Jesus was born of a virgin, lived a sinless life, suffered and died, and was raised from the dead. On the cross he dealt once for all with the problem of human sin and fallenness. Anyone, therefore, who believes in Jesus will become the beneficiary of his atoning work. That person will receive forgiveness of sins and the gift of eternal life.

Paul argued that Christ's nature and work are the dividing line that determines whether or not one is a believer. Everything else, however important, is secondary. In his letter to the Galatians he called a curse on anyone who altered the basic message of the gospel. When ministering in Antioch he admonished Peter because Peter had required Gentile Christians to follow Jewish customs. That meant that the gospel was less than sufficient to make them right with God. "Christ or nothing!" was Paul's battle cry.

Admonition must begin at this point. If someone's basic theology is wrong, then everything else we confront is beside the point—it's like treating symptoms of a disease while overlooking the disease itself.

The second category comprises moral problems—the kinds of moral problems that manifest defiance against God, not those that involve struggle before God. As I argued in the chapter on burden bearing, there is a subtle difference between a person who slips into sin and a person who plunges into sin. Some believers are made vulnerable to sin because of their circumstances. Others choose to sin simply because it gives them pleasure and power. It's this latter group that needs admonition.

Moral problems require admonition at the earliest stages of development. Paul listed the "big sins" in several of his letters (Romans 1; 1 Corinthians 6; 1 Timothy 1). He said that fornicators, idolaters, adulterers, male prostitutes, sodomites, thieves, the greedy, drunkards, revilers and robbers would not inherit the kingdom of God—unless they repented of their sin and trusted in Jesus for forgiveness. Once they're Christians, people need to be kept from falling into sin that remains attractive to them, before "little" sins become big ones, as they usually do. Admonition concentrates on lust, materialism, covetousness, appetite—habits of the mind that eventually surface in ungodly behavior. Admonition addresses attitude as well as action, corrects character flaws before they become moral tragedies, goes to the mat over small compromises before they erupt into big crises.

The third category involves church disputes and divisions. By far the greatest cause of church disunity is self-righteousness, which is easy to spot in others but not so easy to spot in ourselves. Self-righteousness surfaces when we isolate some quality in ourselves or our group—ethnic, cultural, political, doctrinal—that causes us to think ourselves superior to others. The most prevalent division among Christians today is that between the right and the left. Christians on both sides have decided that views on abortion, homosexuality, censorship, pornography and ecology are more important than the gospel itself. Both sides have aligned themselves with a political party at the expense of unity around the one truth that matters most: Jesus Christ as savior and Lord. Such an ideological division is a violation of the unity of the church in Jesus Christ. It puts power and influence higher than loyalty to Christ and his body.

Jesus was absolutely intolerant of the self-righteousness of the Pharisees, who believed that one had to become a strict Jew in order to be acceptable before God. Paul wrote that Jesus' death broke down the "dividing wall of hostility" (NIV) by abolishing in his flesh any kind of distinctive that makes one group feel superior to another (Ephesians 2:11-22). The only thing that ultimately matters is that we know and trust in Jesus Christ (Philippians 3:7-9).

Self-righteousness divides the very church that the New Testament declares is one. There is one Lord, one faith, one God (Ephesians 4:5-6). The church is united in Christ, not in theology, political ideology or ecclesiastical polity. People who divide the church for any other reason than the preservation of the gospel itself need to be admonished.

LEVELS OF RESPONSIBILITY

Who should be admonished is one question, who should *do* the admonishing is another. I have found two general rules useful. The first is that intimacy of relationship and authority of office give us the right to admonish. The second is that complexity of situation, ambiguity of offense and lack of accurate information should make us cautious, careful and modest in admonition.

We are responsible to admonish our closest friends first, not strangers. The reason is simple enough: we know our closest friends best. They in turn have the most to gain. Similarly, church leaders are responsible to admonish believers under our authority. Again, the reason is simple: church leaders have been entrusted to teach and shepherd the flock. In short, we should be most attentive to the needs and problems of people closest to us and under our authority, less attentive to those we know only through casual encounters. What have I to say intelligently and redemptively about the Methodists down the street? A newcomer in my church? The Catholic hierarchy? My responsibility in such cases is to pray for them, not judge and admonish them.

Not all admonition demands a "Thus says the Lord." Forthrightness is appropriate some of the time, but not all the time. Admonition does not always have to be harsh and direct. Sometimes it's best to ask a question and negotiate a tentative solution. "I'm confused by your behavior," we say to a friend. "First you're rude to me; then you treat me like your best friend. Is something bothering you about our relationship?" That kind of mild admonition reflects an open attitude. It invites conversation and mitigates defensiveness. It's appropriate when we are concerned but feel uncertain, when the problem is serious but not critical.

> *Admonition does not always have to be harsh and direct. Sometimes it's best to ask a question and negotiate a tentative solution.*

A prophetic word is appropriate only after questions or negotiations have failed.

It's one thing when we're concerned about a teenager's friendship with a disreputable group of people. That concern calls for long conversations. It's another thing when that teenager is planning to go away with the group for an unchaperoned weekend at a cottage. Likewise, it's one thing to observe that trouble is brewing between rival groups in our church. That trouble requires discussion in small groups and a sermon series on unity. It's another thing when one of those groups is organizing its own Sunday evening service in anticipation of a church split. Whether we should discuss or confront, negotiate or rebuke depends on the severity of the problem.

If admonition is hard enough under normal circumstances, it's even harder in complex cases. One such case concerns parties in the larger church with whom we have sharp disagreements. I disagree, for example, with prochoice groups in my own denomination. Am I responsible to admonish them because I think they're wrong? Should I organize a group to counter their influence? Should I lead a crusade against them? Or should I remain silent and let the disagreement stand?

It seems that in this situation the best strategy is not to admonish but to become acquainted with both the people and their ideas. I could, for example, have a face-to-face conversation with a person of a prochoice persuasion. I could read the literature of the movement to become better informed. I could remind myself that prochoice is not a monolithic ideology, nor are prochoicers evil and callous human beings. Before I ever get to the point of considering admonition, in other words, I could befriend, listen, probe and understand. That's far more constructive than the usual practice.

ADMONITION AS A TWO-EDGED SWORD

A good friend of mine, Elizabeth, was appointed recently to a church committee charged with selecting a new worship hymnal. The pastor asked the committee to review three hymnals. Elizabeth did her review thoroughly, reading the lyrics of every hymn, taking notes on the language, observing which hymns had been included and which had not, and analyzing the hymnal's usefulness to a typical middle-class congregation.

Once the committee convened to discuss its findings, Elizabeth became aware of three issues. First, she was by far the most conservative committee member. Second, she had done her homework so well that she was far more prepared than the other members to discuss the strengths and weaknesses of each hymnal. Third, she was the most strongly opposed to the most theologically liberal hymnal of the three, which the rest of the committee favored.

Elizabeth decided to express her concerns in writing. What started out as a short letter turned into a long paper analyzing the hymnbook around which most of the dispute revolved. She managed in those twenty-some pages to challenge everything that many educated people in American culture—and therefore many Christians—consider "politically correct," including common assumptions about feminism and inclusive language. I read her paper. Whether one agreed with it or not, it was an impressive document.

That paper sent out a shockwave. It polarized the committee, incensed the chairwoman (who favored the hymnbook Elizabeth was attacking), and sent ripples of controversy throughout the congregation. The committee held hearings and brought in experts in theology, church music and feminism just to deal with Elizabeth and her paper. Every member of the committee disagreed sharply with Elizabeth. Some even intimated that she should wise up and enter the twentieth century. One man called her a Pharisee who was "dropping a nuclear bomb on a mosquito."

However stiff the opposition from the committee, Elizabeth managed to hold her own without getting defensive. Word leaked out about her paper. Members of the congregation began to request copies. Others started to study the proposed new hymnal with greater seriousness and to weigh it against their understanding of Scripture. Elizabeth had in effect admonished the congregation to repent of its theological naiveté. She had charged fellow members to become mature in their thinking.

Over the next months the church became as polarized as the committee, except that the church sided overwhelmingly with Elizabeth. The elders called a congregational meeting just to deal with the tension and head off a possible split, which the church seemed to be speedily approaching. Finally a new committee was formed, and it proceeded to study the issues more carefully and critically. In the end, that committee chose a different hymnal.

During the furor, some committee members were nasty to Elizabeth. The chairwoman and her family ended up leaving the church. Yet Elizabeth remained peaceful, kept discussion confidential and did not recruit support. Perhaps the reason she acted so blamelessly is that she, the one who admonished, was herself open to admonition.

Elizabeth told me that when the dispute reached its most tense moments, she lost perspective and became completely consumed by it. She might have lost patience, attacked the opposition, become self-righteous and recruited an army of defenders if she had not been admonished on three separate occasions. The first was when her teenage daughter said to her one day, "Mom, you're behaving as if I should fight, not proclaim the good news about Jesus." That word brought her up short.

A few days later her husband began to raise questions too. He cautioned her: "Be careful. Cultivate a gentle spirit. Don't get defensive." He also suggested that, regardless of the outcome, they not leave the church. "The selection of the hymnbook is important," he said, "but not that important. It's not an issue that merits leaving the church." And then, speaking for the whole family, he pleaded, "Elizabeth, let it go. We want our mother and wife back. You've let this thing go too far."

Finally, she called a friend after having sent the paper to him to get his evaluation of it. He, too, spoke a word of warning.

> You are developing a siege mentality, Elizabeth. You have an Elijah complex. You seem to think that you are the only person left alive who has not compromised biblical convictions. That's simply not true. Other people have decided to express the same convictions differently. Give them the same respect you want to receive.

Thus the admonisher received admonition. She learned that theological controversy carries the risk of distorting perspective, leading to defensiveness and self-righteousness. Admonition of someone else's weakness does not mean we have none ourselves. Errant theology in someone else does not justify ungodly character in us. In fact, it is openness to admonition that makes us good admonishers.

Admonition is the last resort, the final weapon, the riskiest move we make in our relationships with fellow Christians. It rightfully comes at the end of this book. Our success at admonition depends not simply on the openness of others but on our commitment to obey all of these commands. Welcoming our brothers and sisters in Christ will show that we accept them as they are; forbearance demonstrates that we are willing to give them room, confession communicates our humanity, service our lowliness and humility, comfort our sympathy for their losses and pain, encouragement our appreciation for what they do well. Admonition must be the follower, not the leader of the list. We will discover then how seldom we will have to practice it.

Epilogue

I am reminded almost daily of the enormous challenge Christians face to make the church what Jesus intended it to be. What I read in religious periodicals, hear from friends and colleagues, observe and experience in my contact with fellow believers yanks me back to reality when I become idealistic and naive. The church—both local and global—seems to work overtime making its witness in the world ineffective, if not altogether scandalous. It faces serious difficulty in settling disputes about biblical authority, missionary strategy, homosexuality, to say nothing about more local disputes like church architecture, preaching styles, anthem selection, elections of leaders, church programs and personality conflicts. It makes me dizzy to think about how much trouble the church faces, how often the church is divided, how quickly it wanders off course.

None of these problems will be solved easily. Many will not be solved at all. I'm not sure it matters all that much. I for one am not convinced that unity in the church depends on uniformity of belief and style, except of course in the essentials.

Jesus' new commandment requires special attention when believers don't get along. It's our diversity that makes love hard; it's also diversity that makes love necessary. That's why I prefer the strategy of learning to love one another when there is every reason not to. That is love's greatest test. As Paul wrote, love does not insist on its own way. It's not self-righteous, though it must still be grounded in the truth.

Some teachings, like the divinity of Christ, are so central that their compromise threatens the life of the church. The basic gospel is one of those nonnegotiable standards, as the church has affirmed now for almost two thousand years. Still, diversity is inevitable and in many cases healthy. The new commandment was given at least in part to keep the church united even in its diversity. The mutuality commands of the New Testament offer guidelines for how Christians can remain loyal to each other even when they dislike and disagree with each other.

I envision the church as something like a big Italian family in which there is no shortage of difference of opinion and heated conflict. Sometimes big fights break out and neighbors shudder, wondering whether the family will stay together. But when an outsider attacks one of its members, the family pulls together, stands as one and defends its own. They might not always get along, but they still know what it means to be family.

This book has presented a modest plan to help the church function as a family. It has not whitewashed difficult problems, advocated absolute tolerance or dismissed disagreements and divisions in the church as irrelevant. But neither has it answered every question, solved every dispute, revealed the right and wrong position on every issue. Instead, it has attempted to show what Christians can do despite these unanswered questions. It has pointed to the way of love. That does not make questions and disputes less troublesome, only less significant in light of Jesus' ultimate standard.

There is something more important than being right. That something is being loving. Jesus Christ, the Lord of the church, calls us to obey one supreme command: to love one another as Jesus has loved us. No disagreement is so important, no division so final, no clash so intense that we are relieved of the responsibility to live like Jesus. As he loved even his enemies who sent him to the cross, so must we love others. As Jesus said, "Love one another as I have loved you."

Discussion Guide

Discussion guides are supposed to generate discussion, though they often fall far short of that purpose, for two reasons, I think. First, because the questions themselves fail to stimulate energetic discussion. Instead, they ask questions that demand little more than a yes or no answer. Second, because the discussion group itself fails to engage in lively discussion. It could be that the leader is too dominant, or the members are too timid. Whatever the reason, the group does not engage the study guide and use it to explore the context of the book and its implications for life.

I tried to write questions that will actually stimulate discussion. But good questions are not enough. How the readers, as individuals and as a group, *use* the questions plays an equally important role. I would suggest that you consider using the discussion questions for the purpose of doing what the book itself advocates—learning to obey the mutuality commands.

- If you are reading the book alone, consider keeping a journal when you reflect on the discussion questions, making sure that you explore what it means for your relationships and your church.

- If you are reading the book as a group, consider passing the leadership around or, if one person functions as the designated leader, encourage members to take ownership of the group's success.

- Read and discuss the biblical texts, for every mutuality command is embedded in a biblical context that partly explains the command itself. Discussion of these texts is the most important work you can do.

- Dare to apply the book's ideas to your life. How can you welcome, comfort, encourage, pray for and admonish your brothers and sisters in Christ? How can your small group and church put these commands into practice?

- Try to be as specific and concrete in your application as you can. Consider doing one "homework" assignment a week. For example, when discussing the chapter on encouragement, write a letter of encouragement to someone. When exploring the chapter on service, take on a group project that will meet a concrete need. When reading the chapter on welcoming, throw a party and invite a circle of people you do not know very well.

- Conclude each meeting with prayer, not a token prayer but conversational prayer that grows out of and applies the discussion.

Chapter 1: The New Commandment

1. Share some experiences in which you have seen the church at its best and at its worst.

2. What does it mean that Christ was the incarnation of God in the world? What do we learn about God through Jesus Christ? What difference did it make for us?

3. What does it mean that the church is supposed to be the incarnation of Christ, his body in the world? Think of some concrete examples.

4. Read Ephesians 2:11-22. What is the "dividing wall of hostility" Paul is referring to? How did that alienate the Gentiles? Can you think of other kinds of "dividing walls" today? How did Jesus break down that dividing wall? What happened as a result?

5. Read Philippians 3:2-8. How did Paul view himself before his conversion? How did his conversion change his life? What does it mean to "count everything as loss" for the sake of Christ? How can you begin to do that?

6. Describe what your church (or small group) would be like, as concretely as possible, if you truly loved one another.

Chapter 2: Welcome One Another

1. What barriers divide strong from weak, insider from outsider? What is required of us to "welcome on another," as Paul explains it in Romans 14 and 15?

2. What does it mean, according to Jesus' words in Luke 11:42-44 and Matthew 5:43-48, to take initiative and to be generous in our greetings? Jesus used Gentiles and Pharisees as negative examples. Have you ever met people like the Pharisees who expected greetings before they gave them? Or like the Gentiles who only gave greetings to those who returned the favor? Have you behaved similarly?

3. The apostle Paul was a master at greeting people, as his letters demonstrate. Read Romans 16:1-16. How does Paul acknowledge people in these verses?

4. As you reflect on your past, can you remember times you were acknowledged in a way that made you feel important? Can you remember ever being overlooked or snubbed? Identify some concrete ways in which you can acknowledge people. How can your church acknowledge people?

5. The apostle Paul showed that another good way to give greetings is to commend accomplishments. How did he do that for Phoebe? Reflect on times you received a commendation that you did not expect. How can you do that for others?

6. Paul often exhorted believers to greet one another "with a holy kiss." Can you think of appropriate ways in our culture to demonstrate affection in your friendships and in your church?

7. Many of the letters contained in the New Testament close with a blessing. What does the Bible teach about the divine blessing? Have you received a divine blessing from others? How can you bestow the blessing of God on others?

Chapter 3: Be Subject to One Another

1. Why is the idea of subjection so offensive to people who live in the modern world?

2. As the chapter indicates, subjection is the mutuality command that directs how Christians should live in the social order. In your mind, why is social order necessary? How is it fallen? How have you experienced the social order at its best and at its worst?

3. There are two popular solutions to the problem of living in the necessary but fallen social order. The first is radicalism; the second is conservatism. Explore these two solutions. What are their strengths and weaknesses? How does subjection differ from both?

4. What does subjection mean? Do you believe that there should be limits to it?

5. How does subjection have the potential to transform the church (as a social order) without destroying it?

6. What do you think subjection requires from your church, considering the practical problems that it presently faces?

Chapter 4: Forbear One Another

1. What does forbearance mean? Why is it preferable to politeness and tolerance? Why should forbearance be considered a foundational command for the church?

2. What makes forbearance such a difficult mutuality command to obey?

3. How has God demonstrated forbearance? How has God done that in your life?

4. What in your mind does it mean "to give people room" to be who they are? How will the virtue of meekness help?

5. Read Romans 14:1-4; 15:1-2; and 1 Corinthians 9:19-23. What does Paul say about "strong" believers' responsibility to serve "weak" believ-

ers? How will this Pauline principle provide room for people to be themselves? How much room should believers be given? How much is too much? Can you think of times when people gave you room to be yourself? Were you ever given too much room?

6. What does it mean, in your opinion, to give fellow believers "room to become" what God wills? How will patience help? Can you think of examples of people who simply outgrew problems and weaknesses? Do you think people are always capable of changing when they need to? What should the church do if people are not willing to change or capable of changing?

7. Forbearance requires the church to give people room to contribute their gifts, though they are imperfect people. Think of a time you learned a valuable lesson or received a valuable gift from an imperfect person. What kind of guidance does Paul give about such a situation in Philippians 1:12-18? How will the virtue of "lowliness" help? What does it mean for you right now to have a teachable spirit?

8. What, in your mind, are the limits of forbearance?

Chapter 5: Forgive One Another

1. What offenses in the church require forgiveness as opposed to forbearance?

2. Why is it so hard to forgive, especially fellow believers? What factors make forgiveness especially difficult, if not impossible?

3. What makes it possible to forgive? What in your mind keeps Christians from forgiving?

4. What is the cost of forgiveness? Of unforgiveness?

5. Forgiveness has its limits. It cannot accomplish everything that's necessary for redemption and restoration. What, for example, will forgiveness not do? What does forgiveness have the potential of accomplishing?

6. Are you in circumstances right now that require forgiveness? What would it mean for you to forgive? What steps should you take?

Chapter 6: Confess Sin to and Pray for One Another

1. How has the self-help movement contributed to American culture? What in your opinion are its weaknesses?

2. Do you believe that the problem of sin can be solved by human effort and goodness alone? Why or why not?

3. What potential does the mutuality command of confession have for uniting and building the church? Dietrich Bonhoeffer called it the "break-through" to community. What did he mean by that?

4. James associates sin and sickness, confession and health. What do you believe is the relationship between sin and sickness? What biblical support can you cite? What is the relationship between confession and health?

5. Jesus commanded his followers in Matthew 5:23-24 to be reconciled to each other before they offered a gift to God. Why is this so important? How do the pressure to be perfect and the fear of vulnerability keep leaders and the entire church from being the community God wants them to be?

6. Should there be limits to confession? Guidelines for how it's to be done? How can your church begin to create the kind of community that allows for vulnerability, weakness and confession of sin?

7. Why is the ministry of mutual prayer in the church so often neglected? How can this ministry be cultivated in the whole life of the church? How can you begin to develop this ministry?

Chapter 7: Serve One Another

1. What does service mean for the church? Why is it necessary? Who in particular needs to be served?

2. Can you think of a time you were served by fellow Christians in your church? How did that experience affect you?

3. Why does service require sacrifice? What does it mean to have "equality" as the goal? What does Paul say about this in 2 Corinthians 8:12-14?

4. Why is it especially important for leaders to become servants? Why is it so difficult for them? Do you think it's right that powerful and gifted people give up some of their power and neglect some of their gifts in order to serve others? Why?

5. How does service require time? What principles will help Christians to use their time wisely?

6. How can money be used to serve others? What is the potential of wealth? The danger of wealth? What principles of stewardship will enable Christians to use their money to serve others rather than to indulge themselves?

7. How can people's expertise be used to serve the church's mission?

8. How can you—and how can your church—begin to use time, money and expertise to serve? What needs are you aware of right now? What opportunities do you have to serve specific people? How can you and your church function as advocates for the needy?

9. How can you link yourselves to others so that you are serving as a team instead of as isolated individuals?

10. How can you and your church begin to build an organization that makes service possible and helpful? Should strings be attached to the service you render? What kind?

Chapter 8: Encourage One Another

1. How does encouragement function as the "maintenance" ministry of the church? What kinds of people are most in need of encouragement? What does it mean to encourage?

2. When is encouragement especially needed? Reflect on occasions in your life when you desperately needed encouragement. What did it feel like to receive such encouragement—or not to receive it?

3. What role does personal example play in the ministry of encouragement? Have you ever been encouraged by the example of another Christian? What did it do for you?

4. How is encouragement an art? Explore this art, especially in the case of writing letters, entertaining guests and using humor. Have you ever seen encouragement become an art?

5. How can your church cultivate the art of encouragement? Are there individuals and groups who need encouragement?

6. How can you begin to encourage your friends?

Chapter 9: Comfort One Another

1. Explore the kinds of losses that people often suffer. The apostle Paul uses the word *affliction* to describe such losses. What kinds of affliction are mentioned in the Bible?

2. Have you ever needed comfort? What helped and what hindered?

3. Are you in a situation right now that requires you to give comfort? What should you do?

4. Grief is work. Losses can be so overwhelming that sometimes the easiest thing is to ignore or deny them. What, in your mind, does it mean to face the darkness of loss directly? What does that require?

5. What kind of understanding can comforters offer? What kind of practical help? How can comforters challenge grieving friends to embrace life, even as they face some kind of death? What does it mean to write a new story for one's life?

6. How can your church become a community of comfort? What did the apostle Paul say about this in 2 Corinthians 1:3-9?

7. What hope is provided by a Christian worldview, as Paul outlined in 2 Corinthians 4:7-16? How can you nurture that hope in yourself and your friends?

Chapter 10: Bear One Another's Burdens

1. What does it mean to bear one another's burdens? Why is the story of the good Samaritan a good example of burden bearing?

2. What is the "occasion" for burden bearing? Do you know people whose circumstances have made them vulnerable to sin and whose bad decisions only complicated the problem? How has life in the modern world made burden bearing even more difficult?

3. What is the prerequisite to burden bearing? How does that prepare the way for the act of burden bearing? What do you think it means to get people back on their feet spiritually? Emotionally? Socially? Physically?

4. How can your church develop a balanced strategy in bearing burdens? For example, how can you strike a balance between individual initiative and corporate responsibility? Between engagement and distance? Between short-term and long-term solutions?

5. What are the perils of burden bearing? Have you ever experienced any of these perils? How?

6. What does it mean to "test your own work" and "look to yourself, lest you too be tempted"?

7. The goal of burden bearing is to get people back on their feet. What does that mean in practical terms? If you once had burdens that have since been relieved, what did it mean for you to get back on your feet? What does it mean if you have burdens now? What does it mean for burdened members of your church?

8. What should the church do for chronic burdens, or for people who don't want to get back on their feet?

Chapter 11: Stir Up One Another

1. What are some of the big promises and big demands the Bible mentions? What big promises and big demands appear in Hebrews 10?

2. What is the problem of "comfort zone Christianity"? Why is it easy to fall into this comfort zone? Can you identify the comfort zones of your life? Of your church?

3. What does it mean to "stir up one another"? What are the five steps that the passage in Hebrews outlines for us?

4. What did you learn about stirring up from the case study in the chapter?

5. How can you begin to apply this command? How can your small group? How can your church?

Chapter 12: Admonish One Another

1. Why do we hesitate to admonish?

2. What does Ezekiel 33 imply about our responsibilities for one another? What does it mean to take personal responsibility for each other?

3. Admonition requires that we confront people when they are headed in the wrong direction and turn them around. How is that best done? What is the relationship between teaching and admonition?

4. What does it mean to be aware of forces and habits that hinder our friends from growing in Christ? What would you consider to be reasonable expectations of brothers and sisters in Christ? Can your expectations be too high? How do you determine what those expectations should be?

5. What is the best way of doing admonition, as Jesus outlined in Matthew 18:15-20? Consider the three basic principles of privacy, positivity and prayerfulness. What do you think it means to appeal to someone's conscience? How can logic function negatively to make people inaccessible to admonition?

7. What offenses require admonition? Which situations are obvious? Which are ambiguous? How should the church handle these?

8. What does the chapter say about levels of responsibility? What are the difficult cases mentioned in the chapter? Can you think of any others? How should these be handled?

9. Are you in any circumstances right now that call for admonition? What should you do? How should you do it?

Acknowledgments

As in all human endeavors, the authorship of this book cannot be traced to the hand of one person, though only one person's name appears on the front cover. I wrote it, but many people have contributed along the way. The credit should go to many, not just to one.

I want to thank several groups of people in particular. First, to the people of the churches I have belonged to over the years: Emmanuel Reformed Church of Paramount, California; First Reformed Church of Orange City, Iowa; First Reformed Church of South Holland, Illinois; First Presbyterian Church of Spokane, Washington. Thank you, dear friends, for your obedience to Jesus' new commandment.

Second, to the people who told me their stories and gave me permission to use them as case studies in the book, with the understanding that I would change the names and the extraneous details. Thank you for your vulnerability, example and integrity.

Third, to the friends and colleagues who read parts or all of this manuscript: Forrest Baird, Doug Dye, Robin Garvin, Linda Hunt, Monica Holdridge, Steve and Richelle Mills, Roger Mohrlang, Lorrie Nelson, Dave Peterson, Ron Pyle, Dale Soden, Andy Sonneland, Kathy Storm, and Jack and Diane Veltkamp. Thank you for your time, insights and suggestions.

Finally, to my friends at InterVarsity Press. Thank you for your willingness to take this risk and for your standard of excellence.